WRITERS AND THEIR WORK

ISOBEL ARMSTRONG
General Editor

WILLIAM BLAKE

WILLIAM BLAKE

A pencil portrait of William Blake wearing hat (c. 1825) by John Linnell, with inscription: 'Wm Blake at Hampstead'.

WILLIAM BLAKE

Steve Vine

NORTHCOTE

BRITISH COUNCIL

ATLANTIC
PUBLISHERS & DISTRIBUTORS (P) LTD

This edition is published by

ATLANTIC

PUBLISHERS & DISTRIBUTORS (P) LTD

7/22, Ansari Road, Darya Ganj, New Delhi-110 002

Tel: 40775252, 23273880, 23275880, 23280451; Fax: +91-11-23285873

E-mail: orders@atlanticbooks.com; Web: www.atlanticbooks.com

By arrangement with

Northcote House Publishers Ltd

Horndon House, Horndon, Tavistock, Devon, PL19 9NQ,

United Kingdom. (T)+44(0)1822 810066; (F)+44(0)1822 810034

(E) northcote.house@virgin.net and (W) www.northcotehouse.co.uk

The *Writers and their Work* series is published in association with the British Council.

First Indian Reprint 2010

First published in 2007 by Northcote House Publishers Ltd

ISBN 978-81-269-1320-6

British Library Cataloguing-in-Publication Data

A catalogue record for this book is available from the British Library

Typeset by TW Typesetting, Plymouth, Devon

Printed in India at Nice Printing Press, A-33/3A, Site-IV, Industrial Area, Sahibabad, Ghaziabad, U.P.

For Karen

Universes of love & beauty

Contents

Acknowledgements ix

Biographical Outline xi

Abbreviations and References xiv

1 Labouring Upwards Into Futurity: Envisioning William Blake 1

2 Radical Visions: Tractates, *Songs of Innocence and of Experience,* Visions of Daughters 11

3 Revolutionary Prophecies: *The Marriage of Heaven and Hell, America: A Prophecy, Europe: A Prophecy* 39

4 Bibles of Hell: *The Song of Los, The [First] Book of Urizen, The Book of Los, The Book of Ahania* 59

5 Contemporary Epics: *'Vala'*, or *'The Four Zoas'*, *Milton: A Poem* 79

6 Social Epic: *Jerusalem: The Emanation of the Giant Albion* 95

Notes 111

Select Bibliography 121

Index 128

Contents

Acknowledgements

My thanks go to Isobel Armstrong for giving me the chance to think about Blake again in this book, and to Brian Hulme at Northcote House for his helpfulness. It was Frank Stack at the University of Southampton who gave me an abiding sense of the energy and radicalism of Blake, and I thank him for that. I am grateful to the Whitworth Art Gallery, the University of Manchester, for permission to reproduce the cover design; and to the Fitzwilliam Museum, Cambridge, for permission to reproduce the inside cover sketch of Blake by John Linnell.

Biographical Outline

1757 Born at 28 Broad Street, London, to James and Catherine Blake, 28 November. Baptized at St James's Church, Piccadilly, 11 December.

1767–8 Begins attendance at Henry Pars's Drawing School, the Strand.

1772 Apprenticed as an engraver to James Basire.

1775 Start of American War of Independence.

1776 American Declaration of Independence.

1779 Admitted to Royal Academy Schools.

1780 Exhibits at Royal Academy. Witnesses anti-Catholic Gordon Riots and the burning of Newgate Prison. Seized by soldiers when sketching with friends on suspicion of being a French 'spy'.

1782 Marries Catherine Boucher, 18 August.

1783 End of American War of Independence. *Poetical Sketches* published.

1784 Composes *An Island in the Moon*. Opens print shop with engraver, James Parker. Father dies.

1785 Exhibits watercolours at the Royal Academy.

1787–8 First experiments in illuminated printing. Etches *There is No Natural Religion* and *All Religions are One*.

1789 Attends with Catherine Blake the first General Conference of the Swedenborgian New Jerusalem Church at Great Eastcheap, 13 April. Outbreak of French Revolution with storming of the Bastille, 14 July. *Songs of Innocence* and *The Book of Thel* published. *Tiriel* probably written.

1790 Edmund Burke, *Reflections on the Revolution in France*, published. Moves to 13 Hercules Buildings, Lambeth. Begins *The Marriage of Heaven and Hell*.

1791 'Book the First' of *The French Revolution* printed by Joseph Johnson, but not published. Part I of Thomas Paine, *The Rights of Man*, published.

1792 Mary Wollstonecraft, *Vindication of the Rights of Woman*, and Part II of Thomas Paine, *The Rights of Man*, published. Mother dies.

1793 Execution of Louis XVI, 21 January. Britain declares war on France, 1 February. Beginning of the 'Terror' in France (September). Execution of Marie Antoinette, 16 October. Prints *Visions of the Daughters of Albion* and *America: A Prophecy. For Children: The Gates of Paradise* published by Joseph Johnson.

1794 End of the 'Terror' and execution of Robespierre (July). Prints *Songs of Experience, Europe: A Prophecy* and *The [First] Book of Urizen*.

1795 Pitt's 'Two Acts' passed in Britain against seditious meetings and treasonable practices. Prints *The Song of Los, The Book of Ahania* and *The Book of Los*.

1796 Probably starts work on unpublished manuscript epic, *'Vala'*, or *'The Four Zoas'*.

1797 Engravings for Edward Young's *Night Thoughts* published.

1799 Napoleon's *coup d'état* of the 18 Brumaire, 9–10 November.

1800 Moves to Felpham, Sussex, to work as engraver for William Hayley.

1801 Act of Union of Britain and Ireland.

1802 Peace of Amiens signed between Britain and France, 27 March.

1803 Renewal of war between Britain and France, 10 May. Threats of invasion from France in the summer. Incident and argument with Private John Scholfield, 12 August, leads to Blake's indictment for sedition. Returns to London and lives at 17 South Molton Street, 19 September.

1804 Acquitted at Chichester on charges of seditious utterance, 11 January. Napoleon crowns himself Emperor. Dates title pages of *Milton: A Poem* and *Jerusalem: The Emanation of the Giant Albion*, both probably begun while at Felpham.

1807	Slave trade made illegal in Britain.
1808–9	Illustrates John Milton's *Paradise Lost.*
1809	Exhibition of paintings opens in May at brother's house, 28 Broad Street, accompanied by *A Descriptive Catalogue.* Vicious review of Blake's exhibition and *Catalogue* by Robert Hunt in *The Examiner,* 17 September.
1810	Composes *Public Address,* a defence of his art as an engraver, in his Notebook; it is not published.
1810–11	First copies of *Milton: A Poem* printed.
1811	Crabb Robinson records that Southey visited Blake and saw *Jerusalem.*
1812	Exhibits three large tempera paintings at the Water Colour Society, and several 'Detached Specimens of an original illuminated Poem, entitled "Jerusalem the Emanation of the Giant Albion"'.
1814	Napoleon defeated and exiled to Elba. Bourbons reimposed on France by European powers under Louis XVIII.
1815	Napoleon returns to Paris for '100 Days' campaign, and is defeated by British and German armies at Waterloo; is exiled to St Helena.
1816–20	Economic depression, population growth, high food prices and unemployment after end of war with France leads to widespread social unrest in Britain, prompting demands for political reform.
1818	Meets artist John Linnell. Through Linnell, becomes in his last years admired centre of 'The Ancients', a group of artists including Samuel Palmer, George Richmond, Edward Calvert; is named by them 'The Interpreter'.
1820	Prints first complete copy of *Jerusalem.*
1821	Moves to lodgings at 3 Fountain Court, the Strand.
1822	Receives distress payment of £25 from Royal Academy, made to 'Blake an able Designer & Engraver labouring under great distress'.
1823–6	Produces engravings for *The Book of Job* as a result of commission from John Linnell.
1825–7	Works on illustrations to Dante's *Divine Comedy.*
1827	Dies at Fountain Court, 12 August. Buried at Bunhill Fields, Dissenters' burial ground.

Abbreviations and References

References to Blake's poetry and prose are to the following:

CP — *William Blake: The Complete Poems*, ed. Alicia Ostriker (Harmondsworth: Penguin, 1977)

CPP — *The Complete Poetry and Prose of William Blake*, ed. David V. Erdman (New York: Doubleday, 1988)

References to plates from Blake's illuminated books are to the following:

IB — *The Illuminated Blake*, ed. David V. Erdman (New York: Dover Publications, 1992)

CIB — *William Blake: The Complete Illuminated Books*, ed. David Bindman (London: Thames and Hudson, 2001)

1

Labouring Upwards Into Futurity: Envisioning William Blake

I labour upwards into futurity

Blake

This motto is written on the back of a design from William Blake's *The [First] Book of Urizen* (1794), issued by him separately in *A Small Book of Designs* in 1796.[1] The picture is of a bearded figure, presumably 'Urizen', sinking, swimming or floating through blue, green and black water (see *IB* 194; *CIB* 213).

Urizen is Blake's mythological demigod of control and command: he 'labours' to master time, history, futurity, the world. But whether Urizen is rising, falling or drifting here – and his posture is ambiguous – he strangely echoes Blake himself, who likewise 'laboured' for a place in 'futurity'. Yet for the most part Blake found himself sunk in obscurity. 'I know myself both Poet & Painter' (*CPP* 730–31), he wrote angrily to a friend after his wealthy patron, the successful gentleman poet William Hayley, scorned his poetic and artistic work. Despite his fierce artistic self-assertion, Blake as 'Poet & Painter' lived and died almost entirely unknown to the national public he addressed as an artist who believed he was a prophet, a 'seer': a spiritual interpreter of the meaning of the turbulent social and political history around him. As a painter, Blake was largely ignored by the art connoisseurs and collectors of his day – a small number of friends and patrons commissioned and purchased his paintings – and he scrawled angrily on the back of the title page of his copy of Sir Joshua Reynolds's *Discourses on Art* (Reynolds was a successful portrait painter, and President of the Royal Academy): 'I am hid . . .' (*CPP* 636). As a poet, Blake invented his own method of relief etching, and produced stunning 'illuminated books' that innovatively combined text and design in a fully composite art: but though this experiment won him independence from the constraints of the commercial book trade, it guaranteed lack of circulation for his poetry and his public obscurity. Blake wrote of his last, coloured illuminated poem and major achievement *Jerusalem* (*c.* 1804–20) in 1827, the year of his death: 'the last Work I produced is a Poem Entitled Jerusalem the Emanation of the Giant Albion . . . It contains 100 Plates but it is not likely that I shall get a Customer for it' (*CPP* 784). William Blake survived – often perilously and always arduously – from the commercial engraving he was apprenticed to by his father when a young man: and he lived, in the absence of artistic recognition and commercial success, from what he called the 'meer drudgery of business' (*CPP* 724).

As a member of the metropolitan, artisanal class of journeyman engravers, Blake was pitted socially *against* the classically inspired, polite artistic culture of his day: he was a cultural dissident, religious dissenter and, in artistic terms, class outsider. A measure of his vitriol against the late eighteenth-century aesthetic establishment that ignored him – governed as it was by the 'Greek or Roman Models' of English neoclassicism, when his art promoted an aesthetic rooted in the republican 'Sublime of the Bible' (*CPP* 95; *CP* 513) – appears once more in his furious annotations to Reynolds. 'The Enquiry in England is not whether a Man has Talents. & Genius?' he wrote: 'But whether he is Passive & Polite & a Virtuous Ass: & obedient to Noblemens Opinions in Art & Science. If he is; he is a Good Man: If Not he must be Starved' (*CPP* 642). For Blake, the neoclassical aesthetics of the governing establishment – founded on the classical virtues of 'rule', 'imitation' and 'model' – was equivalent to *political* as well as artistic slavishness: for, to him, an aesthetic that enshrined cultural rule and power was in league with a *politics* as well as an *art* of subjection. 'The Arts & Sciences', he declared, 'are the Destruction of Tyrannies or Bad Governments' (*CPP* 636). To Blake art, in its origin and inspiration, was a radical and revolutionary force, and rose from what was for him the well-spring of historical and political liberty: the energy of 'Human Imagination' (*CPP* 258; *CP* 845). Blake, in fact, promoted a republican reading of the 'Bible' as a popular manifesto for political, social and cultural challenge; as he wrote in his annotations to the philosopher Berkeley, 'Jesus supposes every Thing to be Evident to the Child & to the Poor & Unlearned Such is the Gospel' (*CPP* 664). And again in his annotations to Thornton, 'The Beauty of the Bible is that the most Ignorant & Simple Minds Understand it Best' (*CPP* 667). Blake, as he put it in the last year of his life, was a maker of 'Republican Art' (*CPP* 783).

Blake's culturally oppositional stance does not mean, though, that he was a singular or *sui generis* rebel, standing in splendid and isolated individuality against the forces of social convention, tyranny and orthodoxy. For Blake belonged to a tradition: but a tradition that was itself marginal and subordinated in the hegemonic culture of late eighteenth-century Britain – founded as that culture was on the ideological groundwork of 'State Religion' (*CPP* 613), classical learning, empiricist philosophy, capitalist political economy, and military and commercial empire. Blake was part of a dissenting culture of Protestant antinomianism that had its historical origins and inspiration in the spiritual and political radicalism of the republican revolutionaries of the English Revolution and Civil War. That is why the seventeenth-century Puritan writer John Milton, the preeminent poet of English religious epic *and* revolutionary political liberty, was so crucial a figure for Blake – and why Blake devoted his *Milton: A Poem in [1]2 Books* (*c.* 1804–1810/11) to Milton's historical significance and contemporary relevance (see chapter 5). The heady mixture of revolutionary politics and millennial, apocalyptic Christianity that characterized the disparate groupings of non-conformist sects that emerged during the English Civil War period suffered, however, a disastrous historical attenuation in the wake of the Restoration of Charles II as monarch in 1660. The result of this was that the republican culture of millenarian Protestantism effectively went underground – though there was a submerged continuation of this tradition through the eighteenth century, and a resurgence of it with the political turbulence of the revolutionary events that closed the century. As E. P. Thompson argued influentially in

The Making of the English Working Class: 'It was in the immediate aftermath of the French Revolution that the millennarial current, so long underground, burst into the open with unexpected force . . . Chiliasm touched Blake with its breath: it walked abroad . . . among the Jacobins and Dissenters of artisan London'. He adds: 'Against [this] background . . . William Blake seems no longer the cranky untutored genius that he must seem to those who know only the genteel culture of the time'.[2] Blake's spiritual and political project was, in many ways, an attempt to *reclaim* the popular millenarian tradition of radical politics and apocalyptic Christianity that had motivated the English revolutionaries of the seventeenth century, and to make this revolutionary conjunction meaningful for his own historical moment. As we will see in chapter 3, the language of political revolution in Blake *is* the language of spiritual revelation and renovation: for, as he says rhetorically in his final epic, *Jerusalem*, 'Are not Religion & Politics the Same Thing? Brotherhood is Religion' (*CPP* 207; *CP* 748).

Yet it is Blake's place in the tradition of antinomian religious dissent that, troublingly, sets him *apart* from the mainstream of radical or 'Enlightened' political critique and protest in the period. In the first half of the 1790s, Blake moved in the circle of a group of progressive thinkers and artists around the radical publisher and bookseller Joseph Johnson: the 'Johnson circle' in these years included Tom Paine, radical author of *The Rights of Man* (1791), Mary Wollstonecraft, feminist and author of *A Vindication of the Rights of Woman* (1792), and William Godwin, anarchist political philosopher and author of *An Enquiry Concerning Political Justice* (1793). Blake acted as a copy-engraver for books published by Johnson; and Johnson was the projected publisher for Blake's own poem, *The French Revolution: A Poem, in Seven Books* – the first and only extant book of which was typeset in 1791, but never published (Johnson also published Blake's book of emblems, *For Children: The Gates of Paradise*, in 1793). But the extent of Blake's involvement in the Johnson circle of the 1790s is uncertain, and though he shared their anti-establishment sympathies, he was marginal to their secular, rationalist and progressivist creed of social and political transformation – founded as it was on the Enlightenment belief in the value of 'nature' and 'reason' as engines of social and ideological challenge and change.

In contrast, Blake's antinomian Protestantism opposed spiritual 'vision' to material 'nature', for Blake regarded 'nature' as a reactionary ideological category that blocked the mind's capacity to 'create' and envision the world anew. Ultimately, Blake saw the rational deism and 'natural religion' of his contemporaries as secretly in league with the mechanistic and materialistic forces of social domination and division. Thus the deistic fetishization of 'reason' in the period is punningly mocked in his figure of 'Urizen', for Urizen is a rationalist who imposes the mechanics of 'system' and 'law' on those below him, and who uses ideas of natural 'necessity' (*CPP* 75; *CP* 248) to enchain the republican energies of 'imagination'. Urizen presides over a rational Newtonian universe – 'a mill with complicated wheels' (*CPP* 2; *CP* 76), as Blake puts it in *There is No Natural Religion* (*c*. 1788) – that underwrites the idea of a 'natural' social order based on system, hierarchy and socioeconomic division. As Saree Makdisi argues, Blake's language of liberty in his illuminated books effectively interrupts the hegemonic discourse of political radicalism (including that of Paine and Godwin) in the late eighteenth century – for this discourse is founded on an idea of enlightened 'modernity' that promotes the 'sovereign individual' of bourgeois commerce, history as a Eurocentric and progressive 'narrative of development', and the bourgeois separation of 'political equality' from 'socioeconomic egalitarianism'.[3] In contrast to these positives of contemporary radicalism, Blake's art affirmed communitarian identity over solidary selfhood, the multi-dimensional time of 'eternity' against linear progression, and the inseparability of political from socioeconomic freedom.

Despite Blake's cultural marginality and the apparently abstruse nature of his poetry and painting, his art was consistently dedicated to an idea of *social* and *communal* vision: for all its seeming eccentricity, it was pursued in the name of a potential social collective that was, for him, a vision of the 'Divine Body' (*CPP* 145; *CP* 636) of 'Albion', his name for the spiritual form of Britain. The innovative and singular character of his artistic work, indeed, should not blind us to the fact that Blake conceived of himself as a *public* artist, addressing with undiminished energy and urgency the ailing social body of an England or 'Albion' sunk in the self-dividing trauma of war, repression, empire, cruelty, chaos and cultural pathology.

Blake's embrace of a democratic aesthetic rooted in the 'Sublime of the Bible', as the book of liberty not of law, has already been noted; but as well as seeking to reclaim the Bible as a book of the people not the State, Blake threw his art into the *contemporary* social process with a prophetic ambition and political aspiration that, even though it was belied by its fate, remained at the core of his radical inspiration. Blake's very method of production through illuminated printing was designed – though it failed – to make radical art available and affordable to the metropolitan public that he addressed; and we should not forget that, in spite of his marginality as a radical artist to the print culture of his time, copies of Blake's illuminated books were on view in the shop of his employer and friend, the radical bookseller Joseph Johnson, in the revolutionary period of the early 1790s.[4]

In line with the radical inspiration of his art, Blake's *Songs of Innocence and of Experience* (1794) are an energetic critical intervention in the politics of his contemporary culture. The *Songs* launch themselves into the flourishing eighteenth-century book and magazine market for children's verse, and subversively undermine the conventional pieties of children's poetasters and hymnists such as Sir Isaac Watts and Charles Wesley (see chapter 2). Similarly, *The Marriage of Heaven and Hell* (1790; see chapter 3) breathlessly intervenes in the revolutionary dawn of the decade of the 1790s, and, among its many styles, mimics and mocks the idiom of the contemporary chapbook or primer; but instead of a lesson in morality being delivered, as in the eighteenth-century chapbooks, a diabolical homily on the arts of 'Hell' is offered up. 'A Song of Liberty' that ends *The Marriage* may well have started out as a separate work (its enlarged script sets it apart from the rest of the text);[5] and, standing alone, it has all the immediacy and urgency of a contemporary political pamphlet, ringingly declaring in its concluding declamation ('Empire is no more! and now the lion & wolf shall cease': *CPP* 45; *CP* 195) a very *present* spiritual and social apocalypse. And *America* and *Europe*, etched in 1793 and 1794 respectively (see chapter 3), are both subtitled on their title pages and opening narrative plates, 'A PROPHECY' (*IB* 138, 141, *CIB* 155, 158; *IB* 157, 161, *CIB* 175, 178); thus we see Blake *embracing and intervening in his contemporary history* in a manner that belies any image of him as a retiring or reclusive artist of 'confessional lyricism or brooding introversion', as Peter Ackroyd puts it.[6] Blake was a *public* artist; he sought an audience for his art, and he challenged that audience with prophetic visions of current and projective history.

The epic, symbolic, visionary forms of his paintings and illuminated designs may, indeed, have been his attempt to place himself in the sublime tradition of 'RAPHAEL', 'MICHAEL ANGELO' (*CPP* 528) and others, but his graphic work is as resonant within the immediate and 'popular' tradition of contemporary caricature print and political cartoon as it is within the canons of high European art. In this context, it is important to recall that Blake attended the Royal Academy art schools in London at the same time as the brilliant contemporary political caricaturist James Gillray – both were admitted in the late 1770s – for many of Blake's designs, despite their epic or 'visionary' mode, possess the ironic and satiric energies *of* the topical print and cartoon. Thus, in *Europe*, Blake's spiritual or visionary form of 'Albions Angel' (*CPP* 64; *CP* 231) – a metaphor for British 'State Religion' (*CPP* 613) – is depicted in the grimly comic form of a bat-winged, imp-eared emperor-monarch-pope, sitting balefully on a church-throne that itself floats on a puffy cloud suspended in the black night; on his lap the Angel holds open a 'brazen Book' (*CPP* 64; *CP* 232) of codes and laws, and he stares out at the spectator with dull and bulbous complacency (*IB* 169; *CIB* 185). As David Erdman points out, this 'papal-crowned Emperor of Babylon overshadowing a Gothic church similar to the Archbishop's chapel at Lambeth' has a face 'something like that of the King in Gillray's caricatures'; for to Blake 'the pope of British State Religion *is* George the Third'.[7] Blake's visionary art is in this sense infused with a sense of the ironic as well as the catastrophic possibilities of the struggles for political meaning that marked his day; and his visual art is as sensitive to the force and significance of topical or popular representation as it is to the spiritual resonances of sublime vision.

Poised at a juncture of visual idioms, Blake's work is likewise marginal to the dominant religious modes of his time. We have seen how his antinomian spiritual heritage meshes apocalyptic religion with political radicalism in a resurgent discourse of liberty that had its historical origins in the English Civil War, but the nature of Blake's religious symbolism is a matter of complex, shifting, overlapping and discontinuous inheritances. On one level, Blake's religious language (leaving aside his commitment to the Bible and Milton) emerges from his avid reading in the traditions of occult, hermetic and cabbalistic spirituality:[8] particularly such writers as the medieval German alchemist Paracelsus, the seventeenth-century German theosophist and mystic Jacob Boehme, and of course Emanuel Swedenborg, the eighteenth-century Swedish scientist and mystic, whose writings Blake annotated sympathetically in the late 1780s but subsequently mocked in *The Marriage of Heaven and Hell* (1790) for – as he saw it – their social and political conservatism. Blake's own religious affiliations have remained shadowy to scholars in the past, partly because the only group he ever associated himself with[9] (and that only briefly) was the Swedenborgian New Jerusalem Church, founded at Great Eastcheap in London in 1789; Blake attended the first general conference of this group with his wife Catherine in April of that year when, as Marsha Keith Schuchard shows, the London Swedenborg Society was in the throes of a division between liberals and conservatives over the acceptability of Swedenborg's radical views on the importance of 'conjugal love', or sexual experience, to spiritual revelation.[10]

But a connection established by Schuchard and Keri Davies in 2004 between Blake's family history and a shade of sectarian Protestantism in the eighteenth century – the Moravians – has opened up new possibilities for understanding Blake's spirituality. Schuchard's and Davies's work suggests that Blake's antinomian linking of sexual communion to spiritual revelation – as in the argument for 'sensual enjoyment' as a route to the 'infinite' in *The Marriage of Heaven and Hell* (*CPP* 39; *CP* 188), Oothoon's amatory visions in *Visions of the Daughters of Albion* (1793), or the celebration of innocent sexuality in *Songs of Experience* (1794)[11] – emerges from previously unknown links between Blake's parents, James and Catherine Blake (née Wright), and the 'Congregation of the Lamb': a Moravian grouping in Fetter Lane in London to which Blake's mother belonged with her first husband, Thomas Armitage, and with which Blake's father and his family may also have been associated.[12] In the 1740s and 1750s (the early 1750s were the years when Blake's mother certainly, and his father probably, were linked to the sect), the London Moravians went through the 'Sifting Period': a troubled time of 'experiments in social egalitarianism, magical practices, and sexual antinomianism' in which an inner circle of the society 'met secretly [and] lived communally' in pursuit of the leader's, Count Zinzendorf's, 'sexual religion' that venerated the genitals as holy, and saw the practice of sexual communion as a service to God.[13] Emanuel Swedenborg himself attended the services of the Congregation of the Lamb at Fetter Lane when he lived periodically in London; and though he later distanced himself from Zinzendorf's and the Moravians' sexual ceremonies, he pursued his own vision of a spiritually revelatory sexuality in his 'Spiritual Diary' and *The Delights of Wisdom Concerning Conjugal Love*, published in 1768.[14] Schuchard and Davies suggest, tantalizingly, that Blake's parents may in fact have known Emanuel Swedenborg through their Moravian links in London.[15] In the context of Blake's family's Moravian heritage – and the context of the London Swedenborg Society's disputes in the 1780s over Swedenborg's sexual ideas – Blake's attendance at the 1789 Great Eastcheap conference becomes peculiarly resonant.

Nevertheless, Blake rapidly turned against Swedenborg's thinking – as his ridicule of him a year later in *The Marriage of Heaven and Hell* of 1790 shows. But this rejection was not so much a refusal of Swedenborg's bodily thought as of the orthodox *dualisms* that structured it; for, in 1789–90, such dualisms seemed to Blake to put Swedenborg on the side of *The Marriage of Heaven and Hell*'s 'Angels' of political reaction, disembodied spirit and religious abstraction, rather than on the side of its 'Devils' of political energy, bodiliness and revolt – those Devils who, across the channel in France, were at that very moment engaged in building a project of social and political revolution based on *material* and *historical*, not 'spiritual', transformation. Indeed, Blake's thinking – as Matthew J. A. Green implies – remains closer throughout this period to the Moravian refusal to 'abstract the deity [and the spirit] from the world of flesh'[16] than it does to Swedenborg's abstractly spiritual lucubrations.

As we will see, Blake's art, for all its emphasis on 'spiritual' vision, is consistently committed to a project of social and political renovation. In fact, the reality of his art is that – in line with the Moravian emphasis on *embodied* spirituality – he *refuses to distinguish* between the spiritual and the social, the metaphysical and the material. Thus when an author clergyman, the Reverend Dr John Trusler, objected to Blake's designs in 1799 because, as he put it, they seemed 'to be in the other world or the World of Spirits',[17] Blake retorted with the rebuke: 'I see Every thing I paint In This World, but Every body does not see alike' (*CPP* 702).

2

Radical Visions: Tractates, *Songs of Innocence and of Experience*, Visions of Daughters

Sir Joshua Reynolds's neoclassical principle, in his *Discourses on Art* (1797), that artists should use the work of their predecessors as models of 'imitation' not 'criticism', receives this reply from Blake in his annotations to Reynolds: 'Imitation *is* Criticism' (*CPP* 643: my emphasis).

Blake's comment reveals something important about both his own artistic practice and his revisionary relationship to cultural and artistic tradition. For, though he seems to prize 'Original Invention' (*CPP* 576) above all else, Blake's critical and dissident relationship to his culture means that he typically articulates his visions as *re*visions of the influential ideas of others – and the dominant ideas of his world. Blakean imitation 'is' criticism, whether he is parodically imitating (as we will see in this chapter) the discourse of philosophical argument, of children's song and hymn, or pastoral eclogue. In fact, Blake is a radical re-reader and re-envisioner of the mores and meanings of his culture, twisting received traditions and accepted perceptions into new and 'visionary' modes that critically challenge convention, orthodoxy and canonicity. Edward Larrissy, drawing a term from Derrida, describes this aspect of Blake's work as the heterogeneous 'grafting' of pre-existing discourses on to one another:[1] a process that makes Blake's work a dynamic struggle between competing visions at the levels of both form and content. Jon Mee's word for this operation (again drawing from Derrida, in his reading of Lévi-Strauss) is 'bricolage'; for the *bricoleur*, in craftsmanlike fashion, does not create from nothing, but employs materials at hand in order to forge '"a complete reorganization of the structures" that have been inherited'.[2] Blake receives and inherits traditions and ideas, then, but transvalues them in a radical revisionary practice that interrogates the limits and constraints of these discourses.

In his early tractate, *There is No Natural Religion* (*c.* 1788), Blake interrogates the philosophy of John Locke in *An Essay Concerning Human Understanding* (1690); for the *Essay* is a key text in the tradition of British rational empiricist thinking that presided over the eighteenth century with the cachet of philosophical orthodoxy. 'Imitating' Locke in order to 'criticize' him, Blake writes his riposte in the form of numbered propositions that ape the discursive manner of Locke's text. In his annotations to Reynolds, Blake says he read 'Locke on Human Understanding' 'when very Young', and felt 'Contempt & Abhorrence' for it because it 'mock[ed] Inspiration & Vision' (*CPP* 660); and it is owing to Locke's denigration of poetic imagination and spiritual vision that Blake excoriates him. In *An Island in the Moon* (1784), Blake dubs Locke 'John Lookye' and 'Lock' (*CPP* 456) – compounding 'look', 'eye', 'look-you' and 'lock' in a parodic christening that suggests Locke is confined or 'locke-d' in the eye, the visual, the sensual. In *There is No Natural Religion*, Blake seeks to push Locke's thinking beyond the bounds of nature and the senses – past both the 'look' and the 'lock' – and into the 'Infinite' (*CPP* 3; *CP* 76).

Essentially, *There is No Natural Religion* argues that Locke's epistemology is a philosophy of *limitation* that fails to account for and answer to the faculties of human desire and imagination; and the strategy of Blake's text is to take Locke's thinking past such natural 'bounds'. The first group of aphorisms in the text (denominated 'series [a]' by modern editors) is a résumé of the Lockean position as Blake sees it; and outlines the case that, as Locke says, 'Observation employ'd either about *external, sensible Objects; or about the internal Operations of our Minds, perceived and reflected on by our selves, is that, which supplies our Understandings with all the materials of thinking*. These two are the Fountains of Knowledge, from whence all the *Ideas* we have, or can naturally have, do spring'.[3] Blake summarizes, or 'imitates', Locke's statement thus:

> The Argument. Man has no notion of moral fitness but from Education. Naturally he is only a natural organ subject to Sense.
>
> I Man cannot naturally Perceive. but through his natural or bodily organs. (*CPP* 2; *CP* 75)

'*Naturally* . . . *natural* organ . . . *naturally* Perceive . . . *natural* or bodily organs': Blake repeats Locke's word 'natural' four times in as many lines, rehearsing the term obtrusively in such a way that it is pushed into parody, and dramatizes graphically the 'limited' or 'bounded' character of Locke's position. The drift of Blake's argument is that Locke's thinking is a recipe for cultural and philosophical stasis, limitation or *bounded*-ness; for Blake thinks that Locke's confinement of thinking to reflection on nature or sense-experience debars the mind from radically reinventing the world, or the 'nature', that it perceives. Despite Locke's liberal or Whig politics, then, Blake judges Locke's thinking to be a force for social conservatism, for it confines the mind to dependency on the senses: a dependency Blake considers complicit with mental passivity and a powerless subjection, at the level of ideology, to the existing empirical, material or historical world.

Blake's argumentational leap (as he moves into 'series [b]' of the aphorisms, with his own counter-statement) is to suggest that Lockean epistemology cannot account for change or transformation in philosophy or history; for Locke's limitation of the mind to reflection on sensation means that the 'desires & perceptions of man . . . [are] limited to objects of sense' with the result that 'the Philosophic & Experimental' is 'at the ratio of all things, & stand[s] still unable to do other than repeat the same dull round over again'. However, Blake finds the principle of change, dynamism and transformation in human history in what he calls the 'Poetic or Prophetic character' (*CPP* 3; *CP* 75): a principle of open-ended alterability that exceeds or transgresses Locke's immutable standard of 'Reason or the ratio of all we have *already known*' (*CPP* 2; *CP* 75: my emphasis). The poetic or prophetic character in Blake, then, produces the new and produces change – and gives on to what he calls the 'Infinite' (*CPP* 3; *CP* 76), that is, to an infinite alteration of the 'bounded'.

Blake hints, however, that the 'Poetic or Prophetic character' *already inhabits Locke's philosophy*; for when he says that 'Reason or the ratio of all we have already known. *is not the same that it shall be* when we know more' (*CPP* 2; *CP* 75: my emphasis), he suggests 'Reason' and the 'ratio' are themselves categories in process and in flux, and subject to the alterations of history. Reason and the ratio are in this sense part of the 'Infinite'. Paradoxically, then, as Steve Clark points out, Locke's '"Philosophic & Experimental" must itself be regarded as an instance of the "Poetic or Prophetic character"';[4] it is just that Locke has closed off these ideas from change, alteration, infinitude. According to Blake, as Edward Larrissy says, 'knowledge, even scientific knowledge . . . is not something essentially uniform and immutable, but has to be unveiled as part of the historical process';[5] and the motive force for change in human history is, Blake insists, 'desire' itself, a force understood as a perpetual transgression of any given limit, closure or 'bound'. 'The desire of Man being Infinite', Blake writes, 'the possession is Infinite & himself Infinite' (*CPP* 3; *CP* 76). Driven by desire, the poetic or prophetic character is manifested in what Larrissy calls 'a kind of divine restlessness, an endless desire for more';[6] and it is in the direction of this desire for 'more' that Blake pushes Locke's philosophy.

As well as a critique of Locke, Blake's lambasting of 'natural religion' in *There is No Natural Religion* is a rejection of the entire universe of eighteenth-century rational deism that understood nature to be an immense, law-bound material mechanism created and superintended by an ineffable, unknown, divine First Cause – christened 'Urizen' by Blake in his later work. Yet while Blake spurns the 'natural' or 'rational religion' of his age owing to its complicity (for him) with conservative ideologies of unalterable social mechanism, he embraced the eighteenth-century 'Enlightenment' reading of religious ideas as an expression of universal human spirituality; and it is this acceptance that underlies his other 'tractate' of *c.* 1788, *All Religions are One*. For Blake, though, the unifying – or 'One' – principle of religious experience is not an abstractly homogenizing 'Reason', as it was for much Enlightenment thought, but what he calls the 'Poetic Genius': a principle of spiritual universality conceived primarily in terms of the 'infinite variety' (*CPP* 1; *CP* 77) of possibilities of religious expression.[7] For Blake, the origin of religion *is in poetry* or Poetic Genius; indeed, religion *is* poetry or imaginative vision under another name (a position he later reasserts in *The Marriage of Heaven and Hell*, as we will see). Blake writes: 'As all men are alike in outward form, So (and with the same infinite variety) all are alike in the Poetic Genius . . . The Religeons of all Nations are derived from each Nation's different reception of the Poetic Genius which is every where call'd the Spirit of Prophecy' (*CPP* 1; *CP* 77). Blake's contention, then, is that religion should be reinterpreted rather than repudiated, re-envisioned rather than rejected; and the energy of much of his early output is designed precisely to return religious ideas to their 'one source' in the 'true Man' (*CPP* 2; *CP* 77) of the Poetic Genius, a generalized figure for the universality and totality of human imaginative and historical vision.

Many of Blake's *Songs of Innocence* (1789), indeed, seem to enact the energies of 'Poetic Genius', for they offer a spiritual vision 'innocently' reclaimed from code and dogma, articulating a heterodox spirituality that is subversive of the bounds and hierarchies of orthodox religious doctrine and institution. In 'The Lamb', for instance, a child speaker addresses a lamb with questions about its origin that – followed by his wondering answers – mimics at one level the truisms of eighteenth-century religious teachings about Christ as the loving and child-like 'Lamb of God'; but at another level the poem subtly undoes the instructional boundaries it installs. It has long been noted that 'The Lamb' echoes and alludes to Charles Wesley's hymn for children, 'Gentle Jesus, Meek and Mild', published in *Hymns and Sacred Poems* in 1742; but while Wesley's hymn is based on a didactic distance and difference between its child speaker and Christ (a distance across which the child implores Christ to make him 'what thou art'),[8] Blake's poem is founded on a reciprocal or mutual mirroring between child and Christ in which the intimacy between the divine and human is *assumed* rather than petitioned. As Heather Glen puts it, Blake's poem replaces Wesley's 'rational distinction' between 'child and Lamb . . . Christ on earth and God in heaven', with 'analogical likeness': a mutuality in which Wesley's didactic 'hierarchies are subtly but surely dissolved', and child-Lamb and Christ-Lamb are imaginatively fused. Blake's child, indeed, actively and innocently *identifies* his life, the Lamb's and Christ's in a radical unity founded not on religious teaching but imaginative vision:

I a child & thou a lamb,
We are called by his name.
  Little Lamb God bless thee.
  Little Lamb God bless thee.

(*CPP* 9; *CP* 106)

In a real sense, Blake's child speaker materializes 'Poetic Genius' as *All Religions are One* understands it, for he melds religion and imagination in one; and although the child apes the orthodox language of Wesley's hymn, he also dissolves it. In fact, the poem's fluid and internally unpunctuated lines generate a mobility of sense that both installs and subverts religious orthodoxy: the repeated last line, for instance, can be read conventionally as a blessing given on God's authority by the child – 'Little Lamb, *God bless thee*' – but also as an act of imagination on the child's part, deifying the Lamb (and himself) in a flourish of visionary 'Poetic Genius' – '*Little Lamb God*, bless thee'. Here, the Lamb, child and God are identified with each other – 'We are called by his name' – and denominated as divine in a radical mutuality.

The fact that this second, subversive potentiality inhabits Blake's child-like language is a measure of the heterodoxy and radicalism of *Songs of Innocence*; for the poems' beguiling simplicities perform a work of radical cultural critique. This critique stands forth explicitly in 'The Divine Image', again from *Songs of Innocence*; for like 'The Lamb', this text affirms the divinity of the human imagination and de-hierarchizes the relationship between the divine and human. Its second stanza asserts:

For Mercy Pity Peace and Love,
Is God our father dear:
And Mercy Pity Peace and Love,
Is Man his child and care.

(*CPP* 12; *CP* 111: my emphases)

The torsion of the poem's grammar here transmutes the metaphorical qualities of God ('Mercy', 'Pity', 'Peace', 'Love') into the literal *being* of God, converting his attributes into his essence ('*Is* God . . .'). Furthermore, these attributes are designated as a singular visionary identity – 'God' – who is a function of the human imagination. The poem's 'virtues of delight' (*CPP* 12; *CP* 111) are, in this sense, not aspects of a transcendent God – they *are* God.

The language of abstract orthodox spirituality, then, is transposed into a 'human' form, or what the poem calls the 'human form divine' (*CPP* 13; *CP* 111). Like so many of the *Songs of Innocence and of Experience* (1794), 'The Divine Image' refuses to distinguish not only between the human and divine, but also between the spiritual and social: for Blake, in fact, the social *is* the spiritual, and ethical virtues take on meaning only in their social enactment. Thus, while 'The Divine Image' is about prayer – it opens, 'To Mercy Pity Peace and Love,/ All pray in their distress' (*CPP* 12; *CP* 111) – it is not a prayer to a distant God, but to the potential realization of its 'virtues of delight' in social community: to the potential, that is, of the 'divine image' in humankind itself. Prayer is offered *to* the 'human form divine'. This social or humanized vision of spirituality is imaged beautifully in the design to 'The Divine Image' where, at the top of the plate, two children kneel in an attitude of prayer, and two human-angel forms approach them as if answering their supplication; the whole scene is cradled by a sweeping, connecting plant or flame-like flourish that caresses the verbal text of the plate, and links the prayer scene at the top to a Christ-like figure at the foot, who raises up one of two supine human forms with his hand (*IB* 59; *CIB* 60).

If the plate's design offers a social vision of the 'divine image', the verbal text generalizes this vision to all humankind:

> Then every man of every clime,
> That prays in his distress,
> Prays to the human form divine
> Love Mercy Pity Peace.
>
> And all must love the human form,
> In heathen, turk or jew.
> Where Mercy, Love & Pity dwell
> There God is dwelling too.
>
> (*CPP* 13; *CP* 111)

Here, Blake's text repudiates the racism and nationalism that is the credo of Isaac Watts's eighteenth-century hymns for Sunday School children, the *Divine Songs* of 1715; these are monitory evangelical catechisms to which 'The Divine Image' is, among other of Blake's *Songs of Innocence and of Experience*, a scornful reply. In 'Praise for the Gospel', for instance, Watts writes:

> Lord, I ascribe it to thy Grace
> And not to Chance, as others do,
> That I was born of *Christian* Race,
> And not a *Heathen*, or a *Jew*.[10]

Actualizing the radical, Enlightenment universalism staged in *All Religions are One*, 'The Divine Image' rejects the xenophobic patriotism of Watts's hymn – a homily that, in Caroline Franklin's words, extols the 'British as God's chosen people'.[11] Instead, Blake's text embraces *all creeds and races* in its vision of divine and human beatitude. Blake's critique of conventional theology is thus also a denunciation of nationalist ideology. The poem's universalist vision of the divine, moreover, is presented as an active *incarnation* of the 'God' who is embodied in its 'virtues of delight', for where these virtues dwell 'God is dwelling too'; and the 'divine image' is therefore made present in acts of social and racial inclusion, love and justice.

If orthodox godhead is ecumenically re-envisioned in 'The Divine Image', and submitted to the inclusive and transformative energies of 'Poetic Genius', the adult–child relationship itself is reimagined in the 'Introduction' to *Songs of Innocence*. In this poem, a piper-poet is inspired by a free-floating infant figure, who appears above his head as a visionary bundle of laughing, unfettered energy:

> Piping down the valleys wild
> Piping songs of pleasant glee
> On a cloud I saw a child.
> And he laughing said to me.
>
> (*CPP* 7; *CP* 104)

The visionary child then instructs the piper-poet to play a 'song', then to 'sing' it, and then to 'write' his songs down in a 'book that all may read'; and in this way the child tutors the poet in the arts of innocence. Clearly, the 'Introduction' to *Innocence* depicts a scene of inspiration, and the child occupies the place of the poetic muse; in this sense, the poem can be read as an allegory of Blake's *own* attempt to submit himself to the possibilities or challenges of 'innocence' in *Songs of Innocence*.

As Heather Glen shows, Blake's *Songs* comprehensively flout the didacticism of eighteenth-century spiritual and secular verse for children – celebrating rather than censuring, as was conventional, the child's capacity for imagination, invention and play.[12] Wesley's and Watts's hymns among them, eighteenth-century poems for children were instructional and admonitory, delivering adult lessons to erring infants; but Blake's *Songs* and 'Introduction' scandalously invert this situation. In 'Introduction', for instance, a *child teaches an adult*, and the authority of experience is submitted to the demands of innocence. The beautiful frontispiece to *Innocence* illustrates the 'Introduction', and depicts the piper-poet gazing up at the child-muse who dances, smiling, on a cloud of gold wash that literally punches a hole in the dense canopy of trees that fills the design – as if to allegorize the interruption of nature by imaginative vision (*IB* 43; *CIB* 44). Moreover, the position of the child above the piper's head hints that he is a *vision sprung from the piper's mind*, and in this sense the infant externalizes the speaker's imagination of innocence.

But the celebratory tone of 'Introduction' is haunted by the loss of the vision that the piper-poet invokes. For, as the visionary child bids the piper to 'write' – and so *become a poet* – a discordant note enters:

> Piper sit thee down and write
> In a book that all may read –
> So he vanish'd from my sight.
> And I pluck'd a hollow reed.
>
> And I made a rural pen,
> And I stain'd the water clear,
> And I wrote my happy songs
> Every child may joy to hear
>
> (*CPP* 7; *CP* 104)

Here, the language of the poem takes a darker turn. The child-muse 'vanishes', and the poet takes a 'hollow' reed for writing, ambivalently 'staining' the clear water with ink. The poet's ambiguous gesture suggests that he is an agent *both* of innocence *and* experience, for 'contrary' possibilities – consonant with the subtitle of the 1794 collection, *Shewing the Two Contrary States of the Human Soul* (my emphasis) – are inscribed in the syntax of the line, 'I *stain'd* the water *clear*': the line can suggest a 'staining' of the clear water in pollution, or a staining of the water 'clear' in artistic illumination. Either way, the poem puts *contrary* possibilities into play, and suggests that even here – in the introductory poem to *Songs of Innocence* – the darker world of 'Experience' is present. To this extent, Blake's *Songs* meditate on 'States' of the soul, and not on unalterable *stages* of the soul's history; implicitly, in fact, 'innocence' and 'experience' are states that are *perpetually* open to the 'Human Soul', rather than ineluctable conditions of childhood or adulthood. As a collection, *Songs of Innocence and of Experience* is dedicated to the recovery of a vision of 'innocence' from within the 'state' of experience; the poems are therefore challenges to 'experienced' social vision and social conditions, rather than elegies to the metaphysical loss of innocence. As Blake wrote on the manuscript of his unfinished epic, *'Vala'*, or *'The Four Zoas'*: 'Unorganizd Innocence, An Impossibility/ Innocence dwells with Wisdom but never with Ignorance' (*CPP* 697; *CP* 476).

The sense in which innocence and experience are social and psychical *states of seeing and being*, rather than stages of existence, is dramatized strikingly in the first two poems of *Songs of Experience*, the 'Introduction' and 'Earth's Answer'. The 'Introduction' gives us the 'voice of the Bard', but the Bard's is a voice that, while demanding attention and authority, is one of loss, guilt and grief. In fact, the Bard's assertion of authority and command – 'Hear the voice of the Bard!/ Who Present, Past, & Future sees/ Whose ears have heard,/ The Holy Word . . .' (*CPP* 18; *CP* 117) – is a *function* of his mournful vision of the world. For the Bard mourns the condition of a world that, it seems, *eludes or exceeds* his command and control; and he anxiously urges the 'Earth' to 'return' to what he views as a prelapsarian state of existence. 'O Earth O Earth Return!' he says. Eerily, however, the Bard's voice echoes the image of the punishing, authoritarian God of Genesis who, after Adam's and Eve's original act of sin in the Garden of Eden, is heard 'walking in the garden in the cool of the day' and 'calling' to the fallen Adam (Genesis 3:8, 9). Similarly, Blake's Bard guiltily hears the 'Holy Word' that 'walk'd among the ancient trees./ Calling the lapsed

Soul/And weeping in the evening dew' (*CPP* 18; *CP* 117): the Bard of *Experience*, that is to say, is contained and constrained by a theology and psychology of guilt, fallenness and law – a shackled mindset that Blake later symbolizes in the oppressive figure of 'Urizen', as we will see in chapter 4. As Edward Larrissy puts it, the Bard of the 'Introduction' is a 'prophet-turned-priest',[13] miserably promulgating an ideology of sin and lapse.

The creed of fallenness that constrains the Bard leads him to see the 'Earth' as herself fallen, and in need of redemption. But in 'Earth's Answer' the Earth replies to the Bard's vision, and fiercely contests his view of her as lapsed; she argues that she is not sinful and fallen, but is *imprisoned* by and *suffering* from his priestly and punishing construction of her. For the Bard is clearly a figure of patriarchal authority and power – and it is his view that is *in* power in the social world that Blake calls 'Experience'. The feminized Earth, then, is viewed as erring and sinful by a male, priestly, patriarchal judge; and the sexual politics of this denigration of the female anticipates Blake's searing critique of the religious underpinnings of patriarchal morality in *Visions of the Daughters of Albion* (1793), as we shall see. Earth contests the Bard's subjection of her in the following way:

> Prison'd on watry shore
> Starry Jealousy does keep my den
> Cold and hoar
> Weeping o'er
> I hear the Father of the ancient men
>
> Selfish father of men
> Cruel jealous selfish fear
> Can delight
> Chain'd in night
> The virgins of youth and morning bear.
>
> (*CPP* 18–19; *CP* 118)

In a sustained complaint, Earth disputes the condemnatory categories by which the Bard defines her – presenting herself as a *prisoner* rather than a sinner, and affirming the 'delight' of her youthful longings, together with the *innocence* of the 'free Love' (*CPP* 19; *CP* 118) that she feels, an innocence Oothoon will later hymn in *Visions of the Daughters of Albion*. In fact, 'Earth's

Answer' is in a sense a celebratory 'Song of Innocence' – in contentious and recalcitrant opposition to the guilt-ridden lament of the Bard in 'Introduction' to *Experience*.

If Earth in 'Earth's Answer' unpicks the theology of the Bard, grasping it as a punishing creed that justifies sexual repression and oppression, another poem of *Songs of Experience* – 'The Human Abstract' – similarly anatomizes theological orthodoxy so as to disclose its social meaning. 'The Human Abstract' is the 'Contrary' poem to 'The Divine Image' from *Innocence*; but while the latter, as we saw, is a radical revision of orthodox ideas of 'virtue' in the name of humanized spirituality, 'The Human Abstract' shows how traditional Christian virtues are co-opted in social experience into mystificatory counters of political ideology. The speaker of the poem – or of its opening lines at least – is a cynical voice of social and economic privilege, complacently declaiming:

Pity would be no more,
If we did not make somebody Poor:
And Mercy no more could be,
If all were as happy as we

(*CPP* 27; *CP* 128)

Here, the 'human-divine' virtues of 'The Divine Image' – offered in that poem as potentially transformative of social relationships – are conscripted by the speaker in 'The Human Abstract' into a 'paternalist'[14] doctrine that, with breathtaking political cynicism, renders the display of 'Mercy' and 'Pity' to the 'Poor' the ideological justification of their impoverishment. Like 'The Divine Image', 'The Human Abstract' ascribes a social origin to spiritual virtues; but the latter poem utterly reverses the political meaning of these virtues, making them agents of social subjection rather than emancipation. It proceeds to outline the vicious political logic by which self-interested social contest – what the second stanza calls the 'mutual fear' that brings 'peace' – leads to an increase of the 'selfish loves', and eventually to the cultivation of 'Cruelty' (*CPP* 27; *CP* 128) as a ruling social principle; that is, to deadly competition as the hidden or secret driving force of social life.

As E. P. Thompson argues, Blake is engaged here in a critique of the widespread Enlightenment notion that 'self-love' is the origin of social development and progress – and that, 'if duly enlightened, [self-love will] generate . . . civilized values'.[15] Yet Blake reads the logic of self-love as the declaration of social war, for the 'mutual fear' of social contest generates the victory of the wealthy and powerful over the poor and disempowered. Essentially, 'The Human Abstract' is about the contribution of *religious* ideology to this social inequality; and the role of religion in the process is to cultivate what the poem calls 'Mystery'. In Blake, kings, gods, priests and tyrants invariably rule by obfuscating or hiding themselves – and their deliberations – behind a veil of 'mystery', thus passing themselves off as fearful and powerful by virtue of their obscurity. 'The Human Abstract' charts the growth of an obscuring 'Tree' of 'Mystery', then, that by obfuscating the *social* origins of differences of wealth and power, *naturalizes* economic injustice – and encourages 'holy fears' and 'Humility' in such a way that the critique of ideological 'Mystery' becomes all but unthinkable. Mystery and passive acceptance are imposed in the place of criticism and active imagination. This disastrous conversion of ideology into 'Nature' is so successful that the poem ends by saying of its all-encompassing 'Tree': 'There grows one in the Human Brain' (*CPP* 27; *CP* 128).

Another poem from *Songs of Experience* that interrogates the idea of religion as mystery is 'The Tyger'. As we saw, the radicalism of 'The Lamb' in *Innocence* consisted in its dissolution of the difference or distinction between divinity and humanity. By contrast, 'The Tyger' *maximizes* the distance and difference between the human and divine. The poem's celebrated ambiguities, however, reside in the difficulty of judging the nature of the *voice* that speaks the poem, and in determining the tone and rhetorical effect of the questions that dominate its figural performance. For, though 'The Lamb' and 'The Tyger' exist as 'Contraries' in the *Songs*, a certain play of contrariety appears on the *inside* of 'The Tyger'; and the poem's meaning splits, as we will see, between critiquing the sublime of religious mystery on the one hand, and affirming the sublime of revolutionary energy on the other.[16]

'The Tyger' is a self-conscious exercise in the eighteenth-century language of the 'sublime'. The dominant account of the sublime in the period was Edmund Burke's *A Philosophical*

Enquiry into the Origins of our Ideas of the Sublime and Beautiful of 1757. Burke's sublime resided in the awestruck aesthetic response to objects of 'terror' in nature or the self; and Burke found the scene of the sublime in the 'gloomy forest, and in the howling wilderness, in the form of the lion, the tiger, the panther, or rhinoceros'.[17] Clearly, then, Blake draws upon a conventional scenario of sublimity for his poem – namely, the 'Tyger' in the 'forests of the night'. Yet, though the Tyger is a sublime object of nature, the real object of sublime terror in the poem is not so much the Tyger as its undefined, unnamed *creator*. Indeed, the insistent and anxious questions that hammer relentlessly through the poem are unremittingly addressed to the obscure 'immortal hand or eye' that seeks to 'frame' the Tyger's 'fearful symmetry' with its creative power. To this extent, it is not the nature of the Tyger that concerns the poem, but the identity of the Tyger's maker; moreover, the questions that the poem asks hint that the creator who 'framed', 'twisted', forged or 'clasped' (*CPP* 24–5; *CP* 125–6) the terrors of the Tyger must be a demiurge yet more sublime than this fearful creature. The model for the idea of a sublime creature being the sign of its creator is the biblical book of Job. Edmund Burke, for instance, reads the sea monster 'leviathan' in Job as a figure for its unknowable and unapproachable creator, commenting, 'In the scripture, wherever God is represented as appearing or speaking, every thing terrible in nature is called up to heighten the awe and solemnity of the divine presence'.[18] In Job, indeed, God invokes his awful creation leviathan as a disclosure of himself – as the declaration of a divine power that none can withstand. God says to Job:

> Canst thou draw out leviathan with an hook? Or his tongue with a cord which thou lettest down? . . .
>
> Will he make any supplications unto thee? will he speak soft words unto thee?
>
> . . . Behold, the hope of him is in vain: shall not one be cast down even at the sight of him?
>
> None is so fierce that dare stir him up: who is then able to stand before me? (Job 41:1, 3, 9–10)

Here, sublime leviathan demonstrates *God's* unanswerable sublimity – and, analogously, the beast in 'The Tyger' displays to the poem's terrified speaker the unimpeachable and ungraspable transcendence of its creator. To this extent, the questions in 'The Tyger'are rhetorical – and are designed to have no answer other than the awestruck acceptance of the majesty and mystery of the 'immortal hand or eye' that forged the Tyger's 'fearful symmetry'. This is one level, at least, on which the poem's frightened speaker articulates the Tyger as sublime object – anxiously extolling, as he does, the unmasterable sublimity of an abstract, unknowable God.

Yet the distant, abstract, mysterious, fearful God of 'The Tyger' represents a conception of godhead that, as we saw, is rejected by the visionary Poetic Genius of 'The Lamb' and 'The Divine Image' from *Songs of Innocence*, and by the vocal anger of 'Earth's Answer' from *Songs of Experience*; for each of these poems repudiates the notion of an obscure, punishing, transcendent deity, and *humanizes* divinity in terms of the demands of desire and imagination. Seen in these terms, the speaker of 'The Tyger' is arguably labouring under an *illusion*; for he constructs the image of a terrible God out of his *own fear* rather than metaphysical truth, yet fails to recognize this. Moreover, the ambiguities and uncertainties of the poem's rhetoric suggest that the speaker's Jobean or Burkean vision of God is *already coming apart* – for, strikingly, even though the speaker attributes the Tyger's confection to an obscure divine principle, the language of the poem defines the creature's construction as an act of *human* making. The 'hammer', 'chain', 'furnace' and 'anvil' (*CPP* 25; *CP* 125) that forge the Tyger, for instance, are the tools of an artisanal and industrial production – and, to this extent, the poem's speaker misrecognizes a language of *human* production as a superhuman or transcendentally divine one. Ultimately, in fact, what the speaker fails to see is that his *own verbal and visionary imagination* produces the terrors of the 'Tyger', rather than a fearful creator-God who displays himself in this sublime beast. As Graham Pechey remarks, 'in this text the work that the speaker misrecognizes as some god's labour in an indefinite past is the work of the words that come together in his monologue at that very moment'.[19]

Pechey's remark points to the fact that Blake's poem is acutely aware of its own rhetorical performance – aware, that is, of its ventriloquizing of the discourse of the 'sublime'. This self-awareness allows us to see how 'The Tyger' not only enacts, but also *parodies* the sublime; and this is most clearly seen in the disjunction between the poem's text and its design – for the grinning, homespun Tyger depicted at the foot of the plate contrasts clashingly and comically with the terrors proclaimed by the text (*IB* 84; *CIB* 84). If Blake's composite image, then, subtly and self-consciously *ironizes* the perspective of the terrified speaker of the poem (showing him abject and fearful before an obscure God), a 'Contrary' possibility is embedded in the text: that 'The Tyger' is not so much a performance of the sublime as a critique of it. The fact that the poem insists, as we saw, on its sublime vision being a *human* confection shows not just that the speaker cannot establish his vision as God-given, but that there is genuine doubt *about* the 'divine' origins of the Tyger's sublimity. After all, the poem is composed of *questions*; and, while these questions aspire to be rhetorical (like God's questions to Job about leviathan), they are in another way literal and urgent. For the sublime splendour of the Tyger, it appears, *exceeds or defeats* the power of its supposed creator – and it seems that the 'immortal hand or eye' of the creator *may not* be able to 'frame' the Tyger's 'fearful symmetry', or fearful sublimity. The Tyger, in this sense, dethrones its transcendental overlord, outshining in its burning brightness the shadowy activities of the obscurely divine artificer. Thus it is that the poem's question, 'What immortal hand or eye,/ *Could* frame thy fearful symmetry?' is changed in the last line to '*Dare* frame thy fearful symmetry?' (*CPP* 24–5; *CP* 125–6) – suggesting that the Tyger escapes or dismantles the constraining 'frame' in which the 'immortal hand' seeks to grasp it.

It is here – in the *literal* rather than *rhetorical* sense of the poem's questions – that the radical or revolutionary force of 'The Tyger' is realized. For if the Tyger escapes and exceeds the power of the godlike 'immortal hand or eye' that tries to contain it, the sublime beast becomes not a biblical or Burkean *sign* of the 'immortal', but a hellish or devilish *challenge* to it. In this sense, Blake's poem wrenches the Tyger away from being a reactionary metaphor for an obscure transcendent deity, into an image of diabolical and revolutionary defiance. As a figure of excess, the Tyger becomes a rebel or insurrectionist – flouting in its sublime, unframeable energy the fragile governance of God. The image of the 'tiger', in fact, was a key *political* and *historical* metaphor for fearful rebellion in the period that Blake's *Songs of Experience* were written – for, as Blake commentators have shown,[20] *tigerishness* in the early 1790s was part of the lexicon of anti-Jacobin or conservative political reaction in Britain against the terrors and traumas of events in revolutionary France (see chapters 3 and 4 for Blake's treatment of these events). On 10 September 1792, Sir Samuel Romilly said of the French Revolution after its terrible turn to violence in the September Massacres: 'One might as well think of establishing a republic of tigers in some forest in Africa, as of maintaining a free government among such monsters'.[21] And Edmund Burke, whose sublime of religious terror Blake mocks in 'The Tyger', described the French revolutionaries in 1795 as more dangerous and terrifying than 'even the wolves and tigers, when gorged with their prey'.[22] The 'tiger', then, in the public political discourse of the day, became a diabolical sign of challenge to sacred and established traditions, institutions and powers – and it is as just such a figure of challenge (to the power of a lofty creator-God) that Blake utilizes the Tyger in his poem. Here, then, we see how 'The Tyger' – in a gesture of radical revision – turns Burke's sublime of religious mystery and political terror into a sublime of visionary imagination and revolutionary energy. As an overdetermined historical sign, Blake's 'Tyger' is thus simultaneously a critique of religious transcendence and a celebration of revolutionary turbulence.

If political and historical tumult is figured obliquely in 'The Tyger', in 'London' (again from *Songs of Experience*) it becomes the explicit theme; for 'London' is one of the fiercest and most troubled lyrics of political protest in English poetry. The scene of the poem is the melancholy streets of an impoverished London – through which an isolated, alienated speaker 'wanders' to note or 'mark' its miseries:

> I wander thro' each charter'd street.
> Near where the charter'd Thames does flow
> And mark in every face I meet
> Marks of weakness, marks of woe.
>
> (*CPP* 26; *CP* 128)

'Each . . . street . . . every face': the language of the poem starts as it continues – for, throughout the text, a vision of *universal* imprisonment and social oppression is bleakly and uncompromisingly sustained. As Heather Glen points out, Blake's text critically distances itself from that mode of eighteenth-century writing about the 'city' (epitomized by such writers as Daniel Defoe, James Boswell or Samuel Johnson) where the city is treated either as a scene of lively variety and adventure, or as an occasion for detached and 'judicious moralizing'[23] about its social manners. Blake, though, is not interested in social manners, but social *relations* and structures – and the *economics* and *politics* of social relations and structures, too. Further, his speaker is not a detached observer like some Johnsonian moralizer, but is *implicated* in the scene he witnesses. Blake's speaker, like those he observes, is *himself* 'marked' by London's 'weakness' and 'woe', by dispossession and by disempowerment; he *identifies* with the oppressed in his vision of London. He is one of them.

In his classic discussion of Blake's poem, Marxist historian E. P. Thompson shows how, in 'London', the poem's compacted rhetoric furiously ironizes the political discourse of the day, disclosing how the language of British 'freedom' and 'liberty' is actually a language of imprisonment. Thompson points out that the repetition of 'charter'd' in Blake's first two lines is freighted with irony, for while the notion of 'chartered rights, chartered liberties, magna carta' was at the 'centre of Whig ideology' in the period, a political ambiguity inhabits the idea. He writes:

> A charter of liberty is, simultaneously, a denial of these liberties to others. A charter is something given or ceded; it is bestowed upon some group by some authority; it is not claimed as of right. And the liberties (or privileges) granted to this guild, company, corporation or even nation *exclude* others from the enjoyment of these liberties. A charter is, in its nature, exclusive.[24]

Blake's poem, then, exposes and ironizes this prohibitiveness and exclusiveness of the 'charter': and Thompson points out that 'charter'd Thames' in 'London' alludes most directly and literally to the 'monopolistic privileges of the East India Company' whose ships were so visible on the river in the period, and whose vicious 'commercial and military imperialism' was under bitter attack in the radical press of the early 1790s. More than this, Thompson says that Blake 'endows [the word 'charter'd'] with ... generalized symbolic power',[25] for if the Thames is literally 'charter'd' to the oppressive imperialism of the East India Company, Blake extends this colonization of the river metaphorically to the condition of the entire city – so that 'each . . . street' becomes 'charter'd' or shackled to the powers and prerogatives of an economically and politically privileged class. Financial and political power manacle the very geography of the city.

In the terrifying vision of the second stanza, this stranglehold of power reaches into the very mouths and minds of the suppressed inhabitants of the metropolis, for the poem's speaker not only *sees* 'weakness' and 'woe' in 'each . . . street' and 'every face', but *hears* the sounds of enchainment in 'every cry' and 'every voice':

> In every cry of every Man,
> In every infants cry of fear,
> In every voice: in every ban,
> The mind-forg'd manacles I hear
>
> (*CPP* 27; *CP* 128)

Remarkably, the voices of the city here are 'heard' as the *literal clashing* of an immense, all-encompassing chain – with the result that the speaker's metaphorical vision of bondage materializes in sound in the same way that, in stanza one, his vision of powerlessness 'marked' the faces of poverty and weakness with woeful revelation. The 'mind-forg'd manacles' that clash through the city announce an oppression that, in Raymond Williams's words, is at once 'imposed' and 'self-imposed'; for the sounds are the 'submerged connections of [the] capital system' that, at the levels of both ideology and actuality, manacle every mind – exploiter and exploited – in an ineluctable 'organized repression'.[26] As 'mind'-forged, the 'manacles' are, moreover, made both *by* the mind and *out of* the mind in a self-reproducing circle of ideological and material imprisonment.

Harold Bloom argues that the speaker in 'London' is a contemporary prophet who, though echoing the biblical prophet Ezekiel (who goes through the city of Jerusalem to 'mark' (Ezekiel 9:4) the foreheads of those to be saved from divine destruction), is in fact a *prophet manqué*: for Blake's speaker cannot 'mark' the saved but only the damned – and in his vision *all* are damned.[27] The universality of the 'ban' that is heard by the poem's disempowered prophet echoes, says David Erdman, the brutal repressions of the period in which the *Songs* were written; for the bans, he insists, are Prime Minister Pitt's 'proclamations' and gaggings against revolutionary or 'seditious' societies and writings in the early 1790s, promulgated as attempts to quell support in Britain for the ferment of the Revolution in France.[28] Blake's prophetic speaker is thus a voice of political protest that is itself manacled or muted, and his directionless 'wandering' through the streets of the city embodies both a loss of radical, prophetic and public vocation *and* the wish for such a vocation.

Yet despite the poem's disenchantment, its images of weakness and woe embed 'Contrary' possibilities of revolutionary power within them. Among the city's manacled cries the speaker hears

> How the Chimney-sweepers cry
> Every blackning Church appalls,
> And the hapless Soldiers sigh,
> Runs in blood down Palace walls
>
> (*CPP* 27; *CP* 128)

The 'cry' of the Chimney-sweeper is described, in 'The Chimney Sweeper' of *Experience*, as 'weep, weep' (*CPP* 22; *CP* 123); and, in 'London', the sweep's cry of 'woe' 'appalls' the 'blackning Church'. Ambiguously, Blake's image here condenses both social observation and social criticism within it; for while, in one sense, the church is morally 'appalled' at the Chimney-sweeper's suffering, in another sense it is 'appalled' not in indignation but *disgust* at the sweep's wretchedness, turning away in revulsion from him. This latter sense points to a church that is complicit with contemporary social injustices: to the church where the sweep's parents go (in *Songs of Experience*) to 'praise God & his Priest & King/ Who make up a heaven of our misery' (*CPP* 23; *CP* 123). The 'appalled' church, then, responds duplicitously to the sweep's cry, but there is a sense in which the sweep's voice – in the fiercely indignant vision of the speaker – also 'appalls' or *casts a pall* over the uncaring church, 'blackning' it with a visionary shroud that prophetically identifies the church as an instrument of death. To this extent, the sweep's cry of 'weakness' is converted – in the speaker's radical imagination

– into an image of revelatory prophetic power, disclosing the 'black' or malign influence of the church.

Similarly, the astonishing image of the next two lines converts a cry of weakness into a (potential) cry of insurrection. In one way, the 'sigh' of the 'hapless Soldier' is the woeful sigh of the soldier pressed into the pay of the King, and the 'blood' that runs down the walls of royal palaces is *his* blood – shed in the wars waged by monarchy and empire. But, in another or 'Contrary' sense, the 'blood' running down 'Palace walls' is the blood of *kings* – and the 'Soldiers sigh' is transformed into an image of terrible revolutionary power, staining the seat of monarchs with crimson revenge. The fact that blood running down 'Palace walls' has *this* sense in 1794 (the year of publication of the *Songs*) can be measured by recalling the context of the French Revolution: for the French king and queen, Louis XVI and Marie Antionette, were executed the year before, and the fearful 'Terror' in France against counter-revolutionaries was unleashed from 1793 to 1794. As David Erdman notes, 'blood on palace walls indicate[s] . . . an apocalyptic omen . . . involving regicide'; moreover, 'Blake would have known that curses were often chalked or painted on the royal walls. In October 1792 Lady Malmesbury's Louisa saw "written upon the Privy Garden-wall, 'No coach-tax; d – Pitt! D – n the Duke of Richmond! *No King*!" '[29] In this sense, the 'sigh' of the hapless soldier is a cry of weakness that – in a stunning reversal – becomes an image of terrible retribution against the kingly possessors of power, privilege and property. The sigh of weakness is heard – and seen – by the speaker as a vision, and a prophecy, of revolution.

Like stanzas two and three, the final stanza of the poem attends to repressed or unheard cries: here, the 'youthful Harlots curse' that 'Blasts the new-born Infants tear/ And blights with plagues the Marriage hearse' (*CPP* 27; *CP* 128). As with the cries of the sweep and soldier in stanza three, the young prostitute's vocal and venereal curse becomes vengeful, and blasts and blights the marriage and offspring of her respectable customers with disease. Her plight, like the soldier's and sweep's, is powerlessness and impoverishment; and her destiny is to go unheard. But 'London' is a poem about the prophetic *demand* to 'hear' the voices of the weak and to 'mark' the cries of the dispossessed; and, remarkably, the poem embeds within the very letters of its language a cry that, like those of which it speaks, goes *silent or unheard*. If one reads the four opening letters of the third stanza downwards, a silent cry – and demand – becomes visible, readable, audible: it is 'HEAR' . . . It is as if, in a stanza about cries and sighs that go unregarded by those with power and privilege in London's chartered society, Blake *materializes* in his text a repressed call and demand for change: 'HEAR'.[30]

Like 'London', Blake's two longer poems of the period of *Songs* – *The Book of Thel* (dated 1789, the year of *Innocence*) and *Visions of the Daughters of Albion* (dated 1793, the year before *Experience*) – present voices of demand and desire. Just as the *Songs* transmute spiritual or metaphysical categories ('Innocence' and 'Experience') into *social* states of being and seeing, *Thel* and *Visions* articulate the social meaning of *sexual* 'innocence' and 'experience' in relation to their two female protagonists: Thel in *Thel* and Oothoon in *Visions*. *Thel* and *Visions* are both books of longing, and offer 'visions of daughters' that anatomize and critique the social and ideological containment of sexed female subjectivity in Blake's period: *The Book of Thel* at the level of female conduct and maternity, and *Visions of the Daughters of Albion* at the level of female sexual desire and enslavement.

The Book of Thel is, as its title indicates, a book of wishing: for Thel's name derives from the Greek verb *thelow*, meaning to 'will', 'wish' or 'desire'.[31] Thel *wants*, but does not know *what* she wants: she knows only that she is not 'like' those among whom she lives, and whom she converses with self-uncertainly in the pastoral setting of the speaking, didactic nature that is the poem's world. Thel is imaged as a shepherdess like her sisters, the 'daughters of Mme Seraphim' who 'le[a]d round their sunny flocks'; but Thel is *different* from her sisters and is discontented, and 'in paleness [seeks] the secret air' (*CPP* 3; *CP* 78). Thel's difference is the voice of her desire, for she sees herself as fading, insignificant, ephemeral and unregarded; and she asks rhetorically 'why' this should be her lot, and 'why' her destiny should be one of insubstantiality leading to a final occultation in death. She complains:

> . . . why fades the lotus of the water? . . .
> Ah! Thel is like a watry bow. and like a parting cloud.
> Like a reflection in a glass. like shadows in the water.

Like . . . transient day, like music in the air;
Ah! gentle may I lay me down, and gentle rest my head.
And gentle sleep the sleep of death. and gentle hear the voice
Of him that walketh in the garden in the evening time.

(*CPP* 3; *CP* 78–9)

Thel's orison to transience here shows her to be a voice of disaffected pastoral; for she neither elegizes nor eulogizes the supposedly beneficent designs of nature, but haltingly and mournfully *laments* her designated place in a natural order that seems built on her disappearance and demise. That Thel is a human figure who voices discontent with nature's seeming designs, purposes and intentions alerts us to the fact that in his work Blake is searingly aware of the *ideological* functioning of 'Nature'; for, as we saw in *There is No Natural Religion* and 'The Human Abstract', he sees the meanings ascribed to nature as *human,* ideological and social – rather than 'natural' or God-given.

And, in *The Book of Thel,* the voice of nature is the *ideological speech of patriarchy,* for Thel's allusion to 'the voice/ Of him that walketh in the garden in the evening time' hints that her world is presided over by a shadowy patriarchal deity. Indeed, the most persuasive recent account of *The Book of Thel,* by Helen Bruder,[32] relates Thel's situation to the condition of young women at the end of the eighteenth century who, in the 1780s, were the target audience for a huge flood of didactic 'conduct' books that were designed to fashion and form young ladies in the mores and meanings of the dominant patriarchal, bourgeois culture. Bruder powerfully contends that the instructions Thel receives during the course of the poem – from her tutors the 'Lilly', the 'Cloud' and the 'Clod of Clay' (*CPP* 4–6; *CP* 79–83) – insert her into the dominant gender ideology of late eighteenth-century society, for they recommend to her self-effacement, malleability, frailty, unassertiveness and self-sacrifice as the primary female virtues, and rebuke any display of complaint, questioning or 'intellectual adventurousness'[33] on her part. Bruder quotes Hannah More from her *Essays on Various Subjects, Principally Designed for Young Ladies* (1777): 'Girls should be taught to give up opinions betimes, and not pertinaciously carry on a dispute, even if they should know themselves to be in the right . . . they should by no means be encouraged to contract a contentious or contradictory turn. It is of the greatest importance to their happiness, that they should acquire a submissive temper, and a forebearing spirit'.[34] Thel in *The Book of Thel* is, indeed, given a lesson in such meek and compliant femininity; and Bruder argues that Blake, in proto-feminist style, *parodies* and *ironizes* this discourse of the conduct books in his poem, exposing and critiquing the gender ideology that places a prohibition on female 'desire'.

The first interlocutor encountered by Thel in the poem is the 'Lilly', who embraces in her speech humble feminine compliance in the natural, or for Blake, the *social* order. The Lilly says that she lives in the 'humble grass', and reports, 'I am a watry weed,/ And I am very small, and love to dwell in lowly vales . . ./ Yet I am visited from heaven and he that smiles on all . . ./ . . . over me spreads his hand'. Her concluding question is: 'then why should Thel complain' (*CPP* 4; *CP* 79). Thel replies that the Lilly has a purpose in nature – to scent the valleys, feed the lambs, sweeten honey – but that she herself 'is like a faint cloud kindled at the rising sun:/ I vanish . . . and who shall find my place' (*CPP* 4; *CP* 80). Thel's self-imaging as a 'cloud' leads the Lilly to direct her to the 'Cloud' himself, who descends in brightly potent male form and delivers to Thel a sermon about his being part of a naturalized and *sexualized* cycle of birth and death in which, in phallic moistness, he mingles with the 'fair eyed dew', and rises with her 'to tenfold life' in erotic 'raptures holy' (*CPP* 4; *CP* 81). Thel's 'virgin' reaction to the Cloud, however, is to say, 'I fear that I am not like thee': for, she says, she 'feed[s]' neither the flowers nor birds but lives, '[as] all shall say, without a use' – or 'only . . . to be at death the food of worms'. The Cloud's response, with breathtaking pomposity and male condescension, is to assert: 'Then if thou art the food of worms. O virgin of the skies,/ *How great thy use* . . .' (*CPP* 5; *CP* 81: my emphasis). Thel is destined, the Cloud makes clear, to *be* the 'food of worms' *socially*, not just 'naturally'; for his patriarchal social message is unequivocally displayed to her when the 'worm' is called up by him in a vision and appears in the form of *a naked child*, a helpess infant (see *IB* 38; *CIB* 103), lying on its 'dewy bed' in need of 'mothers smiles' (*CPP* 5; *CP* 82). Thel's destiny according to the Cloud, then, is *maternity*: she is to be the maternal 'food of worms', and *not* a visionary or a desiring daughter.

This ideological tableau is reinforced by the 'Clod of Clay', or 'matron Clay' (*CPP* 5, 6; *CP* 82, 83) who, when she hears the voice of the weeping worm-infant, 'exhal[es]' her life in motherly 'milky fondness' over it, and delivers a further homily to Thel about female self-sacrifice: 'O beauty of the vales of Har, we live not for ourselves . . .' (*CPP* 5; *CP* 82). The 'Clod' then invites Thel to 'enter [her] house' and 'return', and Thel receives a vision of what seems to be her future sexual and social lot, should she embrace the generative sexual experience proffered her by the Lilly, Cloud and Clod. Chillingly, however, the vision of sexual experience that she is given by the Clod is *a vision of her own death,* of 'her own grave plot'; and the 'voice of sorrow' she hears issuing from it is a terrifying plaint to sexual war, deceit, misconstruction, jealousy, fear and torment, where Thel's destruction and defeat are assured. For in the world of experience that awaits Thel, the 'Eye' is vulnerable to the 'poison of a smile', 'Eyelids' are 'stord with arrows', 'Tongue[s]' are 'impress'd with honey from every wind', 'Ear[s]' are a 'whirlpool fierce to draw creations in', and a 'little curtain of flesh' covers the 'bed of . . . desire' with sexual lure and denial. Unsurprisingly, then, Thel 'start[s]' from this fearful prospect with a 'shriek' (*CPP* 6; *CP* 83–4), and flees back to her internal social exile – refusing a treacherous world of sexual experience that seems to signify her death.[35]

Visions of the Daughters of Albion charts, by contrast, the sexual tragedy and challenge of a female protagonist, 'Oothoon', who *embraces* the erotic experience that Thel fearfully rejects. Yet, while Oothoon enters sexual experience innocently and affirmatively, she finds herself, in a bitter narrative of brutalization and degradation, exiled and 'wailing' at the end of the poem on 'the margin of non-entity' (*CPP* 50; *CP* 205). *Visions* is a revolutionary poem produced in the same year as Blake's political prophecy *America* (1793); but while *America,* as we will see in chapter 3, recounts the history of the political transformations brought about by the American Revolution and War of Independence, *Visions* tells the story of those excluded from such changes, those who are held in an ongoing history of subjugation – women and black slaves. Oothoon is called the 'soft soul of America' and, at the beginning of the poem, she 'wander[s] in woe'; unemancipated, she is a composite visionary image for a continent that, on the one hand, symbolizes revolutionary liberty, but on the other a continuing repression. 'Enslav'd, the Daughters of Albion weep', the poem starts; and Albion's Daughters (or Oothoon's British sisters) 'sigh [. . .] towards America' and Oothoon herself (*CPP* 45; *CP* 196) in an identification that turns them both longingly towards American political liberty *and* fuses them miserably with American (and British) female and black slavery. The poem's title – *Visions of the Daughters of Albion* – suggests that it presents the visions of liberty and terror seen *by* the Daughters, and also visions *of* the Daughters' own abject condition of limitation and longing.

Rising at the beginning of the poem in self-affirming desire, Oothoon turns towards her lover, 'Theotormon' – to 'where [her] whole soul seeks' (*CPP* 46; *CP* 197). Her innocent erotic flight is interrupted, however, by her rape at the hands of 'Bromion'; and in *Visions* Bromion is a vicious metaphorical amalgam of male sexual violence, slave-owning brutality and British colonial power. Oothoon's rape by him is given in the language of colonization and enslavement:

> Bromion spoke. behold this harlot here on Bromions bed . . .
> Thy soft American plains are mine, and mine thy north & south:
> Stampt with my signet are the swarthy children of the sun:
> They are obedient, they resist not, they obey the scourge:
> Their daughters worship terrors and obey the violent
>
> (*CPP* 46; *CP* 197)

The key contemporary intertexts for Blake's *Visions* are Mary Wollstonecraft's *A Vindication of the Rights of Woman* (1792) – whose title Blake's echoes in its 'rhythm and syntax'[36] – and a work by an ex-colonial soldier-adventurer, Captain John Gabriel Stedman, entitled *Narrative, of a Five Years' Expedition, against the Revolted Negroes of Surinam* (1796), for which Blake produced about thirteen plates between 1792 and 1793 in his capacity as a professional engraver.[37] Stedman's *Narrative* is an ambivalent text about his experience, as a soldier, of suppressing a literal slave revolt in South America,[38] while Wollstonecraft's *Vindication* is a critique of the sexualization of women's bodies and minds in late eighteenth-century culture that employs *enslavement* as its dominant trope for female subjection. Images of slavery from both texts flood Blake's *Visions*: for instance, the physical brutalization of slave bodies in Stedman's *Narrative* colours Oothoon's vicious suffering beneath the power of Bromion and Theotormon, while Wollstonecraft's critique of women being made 'slaves to their bodies'[39] – as sexualized objects in patriarchal culture – informs Oothoon's chafing against her enclosure in the 'senses', or material body. Oothoon complains:

> They told me that I had five senses to inclose me up.
> And they inclos'd my infinite brain into a narrow circle . . .
> Till all from life I was obliterated and erased.
>
> (*CPP* 47; *CP* 199)

Oothoon's complaint against her imprisonment in sensualism is less a Platonic lament for the fall into bodiliness than a critique of the *ideological* banishment of woman from, for Wollstonecraft, the discourse of rationality and enlightenment – and, for Blake, from 'infinite' mind and visionary imagination. Wollstonecraft's version of Oothoon's female complaint is as follows: 'Taught from their infancy that beauty is woman's sceptre, [woman's] mind shapes itself to the body, and roaming round its gilt cage, only seeks to adore its prison'.[40] In *Visions,* indeed, Oothoon finds herself brutally and unswervingly 'inclos'd' in *a degraded female body* by the patriarchal world that surrounds her; for, after her rape, her oppressors – Bromion at the level of sexual–physical violation, Theotormon at the level of spiritual–moral condemnation – name her a 'whore' (*CPP* 50; *CP* 204) and 'defild' (*CPP* 47; *CP* 200). Oothoon, however, sees herself as 'holy' (*CPP* 51; *CP* 206) and a 'virgin fill'd with virgin fancies' (*CPP* 50; *CP* 204); but her impassioned struggle to redefine her sensual body in a language of innocent celebration founders on the rocks of patriarchal definitions of woman's sexuality as polluted and debased.[41] Oothoon's tragedy, indeed, is that she is *subjected to the very definitions that she tries to contest,* for when she declares to Theotormon, her piously self-regarding lover, 'I am white and pure to hover round Theotormons breast' (*CPP* 47; *CP* 200), the very terms of her challenge are incorporated in his language of moral purity and punishment (as S. Foster Damon says, 'Theotormon' means 'tormented of god (theo in Greek)' and 'tormented of law (torah in Hebrew)').[42] Violently and abjectly, 'whiteness' and 'purity' signify virginity and chastity for Theotormon, as well as whiteness of European skin; and

Oothoon is punished for her transgression of these moral and Eurocentric categories. Named the 'soft soul of America', Oothoon is identified as a desiring white woman *and* a black slave daughter. A visionary daughter of America, Africa *and* Europe, her utopian vision that 'every thing that lives is holy!' (*CPP* 51; *CP* 206) projects her and her sisters *beyond* Bromion's and Theotormon's colonial and patriarchal worlds: but Oothoon is nevertheless caught in a desperate historical marginality, for she lacks a political constituency that can voice her demands. A 'solitary shadow wailing on the margin of non-entity' (*CPP* 50; *CP* 205), only the 'Daughters of Albion hear her woes, & echo back her sighs' (*CPP* 51; *CP* 207): her oppressors do not. Like Thel, Oothoon's desire and woe is muted by history; but Blake's *Visions* passionately and prophetically vocalizes her revolutionary and repressed demand for change.

3

Revolutionary Prophecies: *The Marriage of Heaven and Hell, America: A Prophecy, Europe: A Prophecy*

At the end of the 1790s, the decade in which Europe was convulsed by the sublime hopes and terrors of revolution in France and the start of over twenty years of war between France and Britain, Blake recalls the French Revolution along with the American War of Independence, two decades earlier. He says:

> terrors appeard in the Heavens above
> And in Hell beneath & a mighty & awful change threatened the Earth
> The American War began All its dark horrors passed before my face
> Across the Atlantic to France. Then the French Revolution commencd in thick clouds
> And My Angels have told me. that seeing such visions I could not subsist on the Earth
> But by my conjunction with Flaxman who knows how to forgive Nervous Fear
>
> (*CPP* 707–8)

Blake wrote these lines to his friend John Flaxman on the occasion of his departure in 1800 from Lambeth in London, where he lived throughout the 1790s, to Felpham on the Sussex coast, where he was to take up a position under the patronage of William Hayley. The 'Nervous Fear' he refers to is most likely his dread of arrest and imprisonment – or worse – in reactionary

Britain under William Pitt, a real fear for a republican artist who declared himself a 'Son of Liberty'.[1] Britain had been at war with revolutionary – and then Napoleonic – France from 1793 onwards, and was in the grip of government surveillance, repression and prosecution throughout the decade. Blake had, in fact, already been arrested by soldiers in 1780 when sketching with artist friends because he was suspected of being a French 'spy'; and in the 1790s his anxieties about his safety erupted starkly in a Notebook entry dated 'June 1793', five months after the execution of Louis XVI and four months after Britain's declaration of war on France. 'I say I shant live five years', Blake comments: 'And if I live one it will be a Wonder' (*CPP* 694).

The story, however, was briefly different in 1790 when Blake began work on *The Marriage of Heaven and Hell*: a structurally and ideologically 'revolutionary' work that intervenes enthusiastically in the energies of political change that shook Europe with the commencement of the French Revolution in 1789. The text also intervenes iconoclastically in the religious and philosophical traditions of the culture Blake inherited – traditions he believed were about to be radically transformed. On Plate 3 of one copy of the otherwise undated *Marriage*, Blake inks in the date '1790' at the top of the copperplate text (*CIB* 109) – as if urgently to draw attention to the historical contemporaneity and immediacy of the artistic statement he is making.

Under '1790' Blake writes, 'As a new heaven is begun, and it is now thirty-three years since its advent: the Eternal Hell revives' (*CPP* 34; *CP* 181). The exuberance and irony of this 'diabolical' statement is in part derived from Blake's satirical jibing throughout *The Marriage* at the Swedish mystic, engineer and mineralogist Emanuel Swedenborg, whose writings Blake initially applauded but then rejected due to their ideological conformism and conservative idealism. Swedenborg pronounced that the 'Last Judgment' had occurred in 1757 ('thirty-three years' before), but Blake perversely and comically incorporates this piece of Swedenborgian piety under the rubric of his own devilish self-assertion: 1757 was the year of Blake's birth, and 33 the age of Christ at his crucifixion and resurrection, so Blake satirically fuses his own radical career with the messianic and millenarian sanctimony of Swedenborg's claim, filching it for his 'hellish' purposes.

But beyond being a stab at conservative Swedenborg, Blake's marking of '1790' projects *The Marriage*, with all the immediacy of a political tract, into a process of revolutionary historical transformation that is happening *now* – not in some distant future or ideal prehistory, but now. 'Now is . . . the return of Adam into Paradise' (*CPP* 34; *CP* 181), Blake asserts. 'A Song of Liberty', with which the text ends, is written in a declamatory and insistent present tense that suggests Blake is bidding to catch the revolutionary moment of liberation in the very moment of its happening. 'Empire is no more! And now the lion & wolf shall cease' (*CPP* 45; *CP* 195), he declares. Many scholars have suggested that 'A Song of Liberty' was written only in 1792 or 1793 – implying *The Marriage* was produced over several years and 'A Song' marks the victory of the French revolutionary armies at Valmy in September 1792[2] – but recent editors have argued that the 'mood and matter [of 'A Song'] are at least as appropriate to the French Revolution of late 1789–90 as to . . . 1792'.[3] This proposal underscores the sense of historical urgency and immediacy that characterizes *The Marriage*, and points to the fact that *The Marriage* addresses and intervenes in a history that is unfolding exultantly and turbulently in the *present*, giving us a resonant sense of Blake composing the work over several months in 1790 in the heat of revolutionary optimism.

But it is not just political energy in the present that Blake applauds in *The Marriage*; he points also to the *dormant* radical potential of the very forms of spiritual and religious thought that he lambasts in the text for exerting a baleful and repressive influence in Western tradition. Much of *The Marriage* explodes heretically the hold on history of what 'The voice of the Devil' calls 'Bibles or sacred codes' (*CPP* 34; *CP* 181), but Blake's text is nonetheless given over to the *reclamation* rather than repudiation of religious thinking. Once again, the *contemporary* is Blake's benchmark: for him, 'sacred' tradition belongs stultifyingly to the past, and imposes on the living what his secular contemporary Tom Paine called 'the manuscript assumed authority of the dead'.[4] But Blake wants to reinvent biblical tradition for the present and contemporary history, displacing the hold of 'manuscript authority' with poetic prophecy. Thus in *The Marriage* he conducts a spiritual or visionary conversation with Old Testament prophets Isaiah and Ezekiel (after taking dinner with them), and learns that their message consisted in the 'prophetic' utterance of their own firmly held convictions. Isaiah explains, 'I saw no God. nor heard any, in a finite organical perception; but my senses discover'd the infinite in every thing, and as I was then perswaded, & remain confirm'd; that the voice of honest indignation is the voice of God, I cared not for consequences but wrote' (*CPP* 38; *CP* 186). Strikingly, Blake drags Isaiah and Ezekiel out of a sacrosanct or 'sacred' past and makes them speak to the contemporary history of the 1790s; and the implication of this is that that is exactly what they did in their own historical era: namely, declared to their societies the spiritual meaning of contemporary history. Moreover, just as Isaiah and Ezekiel spoke prophetically to Old Testament Israel, so William Blake speaks prophetically to 1790s Britain and Europe. Blake establishes a direct continuity between himself and the ancient prophets of the Bible. Viewing prophets as historical interpreters rather than foretellers of the future, he insists 'a Prophet is a Seer not an Arbitrary Dictator' (*CPP* 617).

Moreover, the biblical prophets – in fact, all the writers of the Bible – were for Blake *poets or artists*. Indeed, his 'infernal or diabolical' (*CPP* 44; *CP* 194) reading of the Bible consists in the claim that it is the gesture of orthodoxy, overseen by 'Priesthood' (*CPP* 38; *CP* 186), to freeze or ossify the spiritual visions of poets and artists (like Isaiah and Ezekiel) into codified doctrine and religious dogma. Originally, the religious text was poetry; thus on Plate 11 of *The Marriage* Blake presents a miniature or archetypal history of how imaginative poetry declined into religious dictate. Recalling the poets of classical tradition, he remarks, 'The ancient poets animated all sensible objects with Gods or Geniuses, calling them by the names and adorning them with the properties of woods, rivers, mountains, lakes, cities, nations, and whatever their enlarged & numerous senses could perceive'. From this creative activity a 'system' was formed – not dangerous in itself (Blake himself was an energetic builder of systems later in his work) – which 'some took advantage of & enslav'd the vulgar by attempting to realize or abstract the mental deities from their objects: thus began Priesthood'. The Priests, says Blake, chose 'forms of worship from poetic tales', pronouncing that 'the Gods had orderd such things' and securing an effect of catastrophic cultural amnesia whereby 'men forgot that All deities reside in the human breast' (*CPP* 38; *CP* 186). In Blake's portrait of the religious mindset, the Priests are the 'Angels' of rectitude and orthodoxy – inhabitants of 'Heaven' – while the poets and artists are the 'Devils' of dissent, rebellion, revolution and imagination: denizens of 'Hell'. Blake's radical enterprise in *The Marriage* is to return religious creed to its diabolical source in imaginative vision, claiming that it is the Devils – the rebels and revolutionaries of history – who maintain the 'fires' and 'enjoyments of Genius' (*CPP* 35; *CP* 182): that is, the art of thinking 'from impulse. not from rules' (*CPP* 43; *CP* 193). The Devils of *The Marriage* are artists and rebels who promulgate the energies of imagination over the freightings of cultural authority.

The radically heterodox vision of Blake's artist-poet-Devils in *The Marriage* is presented in a central section of the text entitled 'Proverbs of Hell', a set of subversive aphorisms that display 'the nature of Infernal wisdom' (*CPP* 35; *CP* 182). While conventional proverbs, including those of the Bible in the book of Proverbs, recommend restraint and moderation, Blake's proverbs are counsels of excess ('The road of excess leads to the palace of wisdom' (*CPP* 35; *CP* 183) is one): but, more than this, these hellish utterances are *parodies* of proverbs, *anti*-proverbs that mock the very condition of proverbial, generalizing, universalizing wisdom. 'Think in the morning, Act in the noon, Eat in the evening, Sleep in the night' (*CPP* 37; *CP* 184) is one statement that pushes the logic of proverbial truism to its limit, taking the *form* of a general moral injunction but evacuating itself of the *content* of any such statement. These joky, disruptive, ironic assertions cannot be systematized in any code, regime or doctrine; instead, they can be read as distillations of the multifarious and asystematic character of *The Marriage* itself, which consists in a heterogeneous array of linguistic styles or idioms, none of which predominates but each of which is part of the verbal carnival of the text. *The Marriage* is a radical verbal democracy, a theatre of symbolic or formal 'revolution' in which hierarchies and authorities are dethroned in a celebration of multiplicity, contrariety, contest. 'Opposition is true Friendship' (*CPP* 42; *CP* 192), the text declares after relating an argument between an 'Angel' and the Blakean 'young man' (*CPP* 41; *CP* 189) who narrates much of the work; and *The Marriage* is the friendliest of Blake's productions, affirming as it does the necessity – and friendliness – of the disputes that drive existence in the Devils' artistic 'Hell' and in historical time, too.

'Without Contraries is no progression', Blake insists. 'Attraction and Repulsion, Reason and Energy, Love and Hate, are necessary to Human existence'. This acceptance of a logic of contrariety – that change and 'progression' can only come about through contest and dispute – is one of the defining features of *The Marriage.* While the orthodox and 'religious' promulgate static hierarchies between 'Good & Evil' and 'Heaven' and 'Hell' (*CPP* 34; *CP* 181), thus holding history in eternal arrest, *The Marriage* deconstructs these hierarchies in the name of a restless dynamic of dispute that becomes the engine and motor force of historical change. Characterizing his Contraries in terms of 'two classes of men' who 'should be enemies' – the 'Prolific' and the 'Devouring', or the 'producer' and the one who 'as a sea [receives] the excess of his delights' – Blake anticipates Marx's dialectic, formulated in the nineteenth century, of the irreconcilable struggle between social classes. Like Marx, Blake understands history in terms of contest and opposition, and sees 'religion' (in its conventional form) as an 'endeavour to reconcile' classes or contraries; but Blake asserts that 'whoever tries to reconcile' contraries 'seeks to destroy existence' (*CPP* 40; *CP* 189). Struggle is necessary, and the fact that this is the case casts the title of Blake's work in ironic relief: the *Marriage* of Heaven and Hell may suggest harmony or reconciliation, but beyond the fact of the mutual dependency of opposites, the 'marriage' envisioned by Blake seems to be eternally embroiled in acrimonious divorce proceedings.

The context of *The Marriage*, as we saw, is political revolution; in fact, the argument in *The Marriage* between the Angel and narrating 'young man' echoes ironically the framework of a key text from the French Revolution debate of the early 1790s, Edmund Burke's *Reflections on the Revolution in France* (1790). Burke's text – an attack on the Revolution's explosion of everything, for him, sacred in political order and social tradition – is written in the form of a letter of warning to a 'very young gentleman at Paris' about the nature of 'the hot spirit drawn out of the alembick of hell, which in France is now furiously boiling'.[5] Burke uses the rhetoric of 'hell' to characterize and demonize the rising of the Revolution: and the Burkian Angel in Blake's *Marriage*, warning the young man about the 'hot burning dungeon' he is heading for, likewise calls up a hellish image of terror when he depicts the young man's 'eternal lot'. The young man reports the Angel's vision:

> beneath us was nothing now to be seen but a black tempest, till looking east between the clouds & the waves. we saw a cataract of blood mixed with fire and not many stones throw from us appeard and sunk again the scaly fold of a monstrous serpent. at last to the east, distant about three degrees appear a fiery crest above the waves . . . it was the head of Leviathan, his forehead was divided into streaks of green & purple like those on a tigers forehead: soon we saw his mouth & red gills hang just above the raging foam tinging the black deep with beams of blood, advancing toward us with all the fury of a spiritual existence. (*CPP* 41; *CP* 190–91)

David Erdman writes that the position from which Leviathan rises – 'to the east, distant about three degrees' – is 'about the distance of Paris from London',[6] and this shows how the fearful picture the Angel is invoking is both a monstrous Burkian perception of revolution *and* a terrifying vision of avenging or punishing Godhead, bearing down on the young man with unstoppable and bloodthirsty vengeance.

Yet this Burkian or 'Angelic' perspective on Revolution (and on God) is not the whole story; for, after the vision of Leviathan vanishes, the Angel leaves, and the young man finds himself 'sitting on a pleasant bank beside a river by moon light hearing a harper who sung to the harp . . .' The young man catches up with the Angel, and says, 'All that we saw was owing to your metaphysics: for when you ran away, I found myself on a bank by moonlight hearing a harper' (*CPP* 41; *CP* 191). The scene shifts from the terrifyingly sublime to the delightfully beautiful;[7] and Blake's ironic vignette thus draws attention to the way in which political and ideological *perspective*, not intrinsic truth, governs the vision of history, and how Godhead – and Heaven and Hell – are functions of human rather than divine envisioning. Blake's narrator makes the same point in terms of theology and aesthetics when he comments archly on Plate 6, 'As I was walking among the fires of hell, delighted with the enjoyments of Genius; which to Angels look like torment and insanity. I collected some of their Proverbs . . .' (*CPP* 35; *CP* 182). The 'fires of hell', Blake asserts, only 'look like' torment and insanity from the Angels' point of view: from the perspective of Hell, these fires are the flames of creativity, and Hell's 'insanity' is the exuberance of ungovernable artistic genius. Blake's 'Hell' is not a place of eternal torment, but of uncontrollable imaginative (and political) potential.

'A Song of Liberty' with which *The Marriage* ends sublimely invokes the birth of a 'new born terror' on the scene of history – also called a 'new born fire', 'new born wonder' and 'son of fire' (*CPP* 44–5; *CP* 194–5). 'A Song' returns to the shadowy prophetic mode with which *The Marriage* began (see 'The Argument': *CPP* 33; *CP* 180), but instead of 'Rintrah' adumbrating revolutionary change as in 'The Argument', a new character emerges – a fiery insurrectionist who is not named in 'A Song', but is identified in *America: A Prophecy* (1793) as 'Orc'. Orc is Blake's avatar of rebellion and revolt in history, a mythological signifier of revolutionary challenge, change and convulsion. He appears in *America* at the same time that, in the early 1790s, Blake's treatment of contemporary historical processes shifts from the formal heterogeneity of *The Marriage* to the genre of sustained poetic and visionary prophecy. In this new idiom, empirical historical characters are increasingly supplanted by mythological or symbolic representations of psychical, historical and ideological forces. *America* – which allegorizes the ideological war of the American Revolution and American War of Independence of 1775–83 – leaves behind the residual referentiality of the fragmentary *The French Revolution* (1791), and presents spiritual agencies (alongside attenuated historical figures) as constitutive of the movements of human history.

In contrast to *The Marriage* and *The French Revolution* – each of which embodies what David Bindman calls the 'exultant radicalism of the years 1789–91', and 'the belief that the irresistible logic of revolution would imminently conquer Britain'[8] – *America* is a markedly darker work. Printed in the latter part of 1793, the poem was produced in a year of dramatic and traumatic historical change both in France and Britain: the French king was executed at the end of January, Britain declared war on France at the start of February, and the bloody Reign of Terror under Robespierre began in September. In this terrible and terrifying context, Blake looks back to the American Revolution of the late 1770s, as if stuggling to resee in America's political victory of a decade before the promise of liberty in Britain and Europe now. The widespread belief that America's revolution would spread to all nations had – as yet – failed to materialize, and Blake's revisiting of America in the 1790s thus represents an attempt to *reclaim* that past for the present and future. As Detlef Dörrbecker says, Blake takes 'the history of the immediate past . . . as an exemplum with a view toward the future'.[9]

More than this, Blake passionately builds a 'prophetic' reading of history in *America* that – in a context of turbulence and struggle – strives to grasp the tumult of contemporary history in terms of the future-oriented structures of biblical typology. As recent historicist commentators have demonstrated comprehensively, Blake's view of history in the 1790s belonged to a marginal, dissenting tradition of millenarian radicalism that read the biblical book of Revelation as 'being fulfilled in contemporary events';[10] that is to say, saw the political revolutions of the time as the fulfilment of biblical prophecies of the end of oppression, war and injustice in the historical establishment of a millennium of peace, justice and liberty. This means that Blake's use of religious language and rhetoric in his prophetic books is not an *evasion* of politics or history, but *is* the political language that he employs. The prophetic books of the 1790s are, then, part of Blake's 'Bible of Hell' announced in *The Marriage*, for they make good a reading of the Bible 'in its infernal or diabolical sense' (*CPP* 44; *CP* 194), construing the Bible as a prophetic text about *historical* rather than abstractly spiritual or metaphysical regeneration. Consequently, as David E. James argues, it is an error to read Blake's prophecies in terms of the 'bifurcation of human experience into soul (good) and body (evil) upon which any distinction between spiritual and political revolution could be based': for in the figure of Orc 'values that we conventionally isolate into the separate realms of religion and politics are unified and identified'. James adds: 'the terms by which [Orc] is defined in [*America*] reveal political revolution as coincident with spiritual and aesthetic revolution'.[11] In this sense, Orc promises the renovation of the spirit *and* body; for his revolution pulverizes both the oppressive moral law ('The fiery joy, that Urizen perverted to ten commands,/ . . . That stony law I stamp to dust', he says (*CPP* 54; *CP* 213)) and brutally oppressive historical practices ('Let the slave grinding at the mill, run out into the field:/ Let him look up into the heavens & laugh in the bright air', he sings (*CPP* 53; *CP* 212)). Orcian revolution overrides the opposition of spirituality and history, refuting the idealist and dualist severance of soul from body.

But what Orc *promises* in *America* is not fulfilled in the historical scene of Blake's prophecy. Rather, Orc's energy belongs to a history of ongoing and unresolved strife. His story is one of ambivalence and indeterminacy that allegorizes nothing short of the *struggle* of liberatory and emancipatory vision to take on a determinate historical form. Thus in both *America* and the poem that accompanies it, *Europe: A Prophecy* (1794), Blake envisions Orc in troubled, perilous and traumatic contest with the historical forces that threaten to extinguish or efface him. Orc's first manifestation in the 'Preludium' to *America* associates him with the indeterminate rhetoric of the sublime, for he is a figural shape-shifter whose obscure harrying and then violation of the 'shadowy daughter of Urthona' (*CPP* 52; *CP* 208) at the beginning of the text keeps him disconcertingly *beyond* stable or unambiguous identifications. Orc embodies the meaning of a revolutionary event that will change history forever, but the 'daughter of Urthona' cannot recognize in him any fixed or identifiable form. Instead, the 'daughter' – who can be read herself as an obscure figure of potential theatres of revolutionary change beyond 'America' – sees Orc variously and unstably as 'the image of God who dwells in darkness of Africa', as 'struggling afflictions' endured darkly on her 'American plains', as 'a serpent in Canada, who courts me to his love', as 'In Mexico an Eagle . . . a Lion in Peru', and as 'a Whale in the South-sea, drinking my soul away' (*CPP* 52; *CP* 209). Orc's revolutionary emergence, then, is figured in terms of a sublime potentiality and traumatic indeterminacy that points to the possibility but not certitude of a general emancipatory renovation; Orc's revolution remains disconcertingly *future*-directed.

For the 'daughter of *Urth-ona*' – who, punningly, is the subjected daughter of the shadowy patriarchal 'owner' of 'Earth', a 'father stern' (*CPP* 51; *CP* 208) – Orc's convulsive rising is ambivalently a liberation *and* violation. Tended and fed by the daughter when chained, Orc breaks free and violently rapes her when released (see *CPP* 52; *CP* 209); and this brutal attack bespeaks the limits as well as possibilities of Orc's liberating force, for his 'triumphant phallogocentrism'[12] leaves the *sexual* politics of the American continent untransformed and unrevolutionized. Indeed, Orc is a figure of what Terry Eagleton (in another context) calls Blake's 'revolutionary ambiguity'.[13] Blake's awareness of the contradictoriness of Orcian revolution is hinted at in his production – in the same year as *America* – of *Visions of the Daughters of Albion* (1793), a feminist addendum to *America* which, as we saw in chapter 2, movingly depicts the fate of Oothoon, the 'soft soul of America' (*CPP* 45; *CP* 196), who is enchained in an ongoing history of sexual and racial subjection. Oothoon is brutally raped like the 'daughter of Urthona', but she lacks any political constituency to voice her demands or desires; and she is *not* spoken for by the phallic Orc. The American Revolution that Orc superintends is, instead, one of 'warlike *men*' – of 'Brothers & sons of America' (*CPP* 52; *CP* 210: my emphasis), rather than sisters or 'daughters'. Further, as Saree Makdisi points out, the rebels and leaders of the American War (mythologically personified in Orc) were bourgeois political radicals on the one hand, but *slave-owning*[14] citizens on the other. In spite of Orc's call to the slave to 'run out into the field', then, political revolution in *America* leaves sexual subjection and black slavery in place. As we saw, *Visions of the Daughters of Albion* mournfully encodes, in the unheared lamentations of Oothoon on the 'margin' of historical 'non-entity' (*CPP* 50; *CP* 205), the two vicious subjections that Orc's American revolution leaves untouched: those 'obliterated and erased' (*CPP* 47; *CP* 199) from revolutionary history by race and sex.

The 'Preludium' to *America* ends with the daughter of Urthona wailing in the torments of historical change. She says:

> O what limb rending pains I feel, thy fire & my frost
> Mingle in howling pains, in furrows by thy lightnings rent;
> This is eternal death; and this the torment long foretold.
>
> (*CPP* 52; *CP* 209–10)

The trauma of transformation endured by the daughter here suggests that the 'mingling' of her story with Orc's – the confusion of 'fire' and 'frost', revolution and reaction, rebellion and repression – suspends revolutionary birth in a struggle in which regeneration dissolves in 'eternal death'. This indeterminate suspension of revolutionary realization irrupts metafictionally in Blake's text when, under these lines, he etches the following words that compound the traumatic incertitude of Orc's rising:

> The stern Bard ceas'd, asham'd of his own song; enrag'd he swung
> His harp aloft sounding, then dash'd its shining frame against
> A ruin'd pillar in glittring fragments; silent he turn'd away,
> And wander'd down the vales of Kent in sick & drear lamentings.
>
> (*CPP* 52; *CP* 210)

Although these lines are usually taken to be a sign of Blake's fluctuating revolutionary hopes – a marker of his scepticism in the early 1790s about the prospects of Orcian revolution – the fact that he *masked* the lines in all but two of the thirteen copies he printed of *America,* suggests that Blake *embraced* the indeterminacy of Orc as a historical sign at the same time as he anatomized the contradictions comprising his revolutionary 'terror' (*CPP* 54; *CP* 213).

The terrible or sublime uncertainty attending Orc's eruption in history is graphically marked on Plate 7 of *America* when, at the foot of a passage describing Orc as a serpentine 'Spectre' who 'stain[s] the temple long/ With beams of blood' (*CPP* 53; *CP* 212), Blake etches an immense, coiled serpent rising up in the shape of an overwhelming and engulfing *question mark* (*IB* 143; *CIB* 160). Yet the question – and question mark – of Orc's historical signification in *America* is one to which the struggling figures of Blake's poem (and of his other 1790s prophecies and books) fail to provide an answer. For the sublime convulsions of the revolutionary historical process in Blake's 1790s works bear witness to a history that, as we have seen, is increasingly inscribed less in a rhetoric of transformation than of trauma. Like the 'spectre of Communism' that, half a century later, Marx and Engels will announce is 'haunting Europe',[15] the 'Spectre' of Orcian revolution traumatizes history with the force of the new, the unprecedented, the incalculable. Orc is the sign of a future and, as yet, unrealized liberation; and his historical indeterminacy renders him uncontainable at the level both of event and of rhetorical presentation. He represents a 'sublime' infraction of political and representational structures.

Most of *America* is devoted, in fact, not to narrating the American Revolution and the subsequent War of Independence, but to a conspectus of competing 'visions' or representations of Orc's revolt and the doomed repression of it by 'Albion' (Britain). As the American rebels – 'Washington, Franklin, Paine & Warren, Gates, Hancock & Green' – gather on the coast and 'look over the Atlantic sea', they see a vision of 'Albions wrathful Prince' (King George III):

> a terrible blast swept over the heaving sea;
> The eastern cloud rent; on his cliffs stood Albions wrathful Prince
> A dragon form clashing his scales at midnight he arose,
> And flam'd red meteors round the land of Albion beneath[.]
> His voice, his locks, his awful shoulders, and his glowing eyes,
> Appear to the Americans upon the cloudy night.
>
> (*CPP* 52–3; *CP* 211)

'*Appear to the Americans* upon the cloudy night': Blake's narrative rhetoric presents history as a spiritual vision or appearance, rather than simply a literal event, for Albion's Prince raises himself up as a 'dragon form' to terrify the Americans. Albion's Prince appears as a dragon form *to the Americans* because, as their baleful oppressor, that is what he *is* to them, for in *America* vision is history and history is vision. Blake's visionary rhetoric depicts history, then, in its conflicted and contested spiritual or imaginative forms – giving the 'historical fact in its poetical vigour', as he puts it in *A Descriptive Catalogue* (1809). Blake's history is one of 'miracle or prodigy' – a *visionary* history – rather than of the 'dull round of probabilities and possibilities' that is empirical history (*CPP* 543). Thus in *America* Albion's Angel has a vision of Orc that bears all the marks of an 'Angelic' vision of political rebellion, suffused as it is with the language of orthodox demonology and the iconography of sin:

> Art thou not Orc; who serpent-form'd
> Stands at the gate of Enitharmon to devour her children;
> Blasphemous Demon, Antichrist, hater of Dignities;
> Lover of wild rebellion, and transgressor of God's Law;
> Why dost thou come to Angels eyes in this terrific form?
>
> (*CPP* 53–4; *CP* 213)

'Why dost thou come *to Angels eyes* in this terrific form': Blake's language indicates that this is how revolution appears 'to' the Angel – as the demonic desecrator of Law. As in the dispute between the Angel and the young man in *The Marriage of Heaven and Hell*, Albion's Angels and America's rebels construct the world – and history – differently; and in many ways *America* is a gallery of antagonistic visions that presents revolution as an immense or sublime Orcian *question mark* over whose meaning the antagonists in the poem struggle, and for which the text strives to find an adequate image. But sublime indeterminacy conditions Blake's presentation of revolutionary history even in the space of a single illuminated plate and its colouring. Thus on Plate 12 (*IB* 148; *CIB* 165) Blake presents the figure of Orc surrounded by flames, and his fiery pose mimics and mocks the cloudy and miserably transcendent posture of 'Urizen' – Blake's demigod of political reaction – two plates before (*IB* 146; *CIB* 163). The relationship between the two plates is one of both contest and mirroring, for these Blakean figures are antagonists yet also locked in mutually constitutive struggle. What is significant, though, is the indeterminacy that structures the image on Plate 12: the ambiguity of whether Orc is rising in fiery birth to depose the cloudy Urizen, or whether he is in fact being engulfed by the very flames that fold about him[16] – whether the image, that is, is one of his consummation or immolation, emergence or obliteration.

In *America* Blake recalls, as we saw, the revolutionary and victorious America of the 1770s and 1780s in order to understand the turbulent moment of revolutionary struggle in France and Europe in the early 1790s: the poem seeks to reclaim America's emancipation from 'Empire' (*CPP* 53; *CP* 212) *prophetically* so as to grasp the meaning of the fearful contemporary theatre of revolution in France in 1793. Like much radical discourse of the period, *America* envisions the transmigration of revolution (in the shape of Orc) from the American to the European continents. At the end of *America*, Urizen seeks to hide the fires of Orc from the earth, but manages to do so only temporarily until the time 'when France receiv'd the Demons light' (*CPP* 57; *CP* 221); and France or Europe is the scene of Blake's next revolutionary poem, *Europe: A Prophecy* (1794).

Europe places itself directly in the context of the French Revolution; but it is a much darker and more troubled vision of revolution than *America*. While *America* revisits the recent revolutionary past, *Europe* confronts the *present* of contemporary history – or at least seems to from its declamatory title. Yet in another sense *Europe* (like *America*, which looks *back* from the 1790s) turns its vision away from the immediacy of the political present, and meditates on the nightmarish *pre*history of contemporary events. In fact, the poem revisits the entire history of western Christendom in order to take the measure of the history and ideology of state Christianity that the French Revolution opposes. Like *America*, the narrative of *Europe* is prefaced by a 'Preludium' that presents Orc and the 'nameless shadowy female' (*CPP* 60; *CP* 226) in tortured embrace, but the focus is now on the lamenting female rather than the rising Orc. If the 'daughter of Urthona' in *America* seems to figure potential theatres of future revolutionary history, the nameless female in *Europe* images the hopeless repetition of an enslaved and tormented past; and *Europe* unfolds against the traumatic backdrop of endlessly repeated war between obscurely embattled powers – between revolutionary 'howling terrors' (echoing Orc) and 'all devouring fiery kings' (echoing Urizen (*CPP* 61, *CP* 227)). As Helen Bruder says, these remorseless historical forces appear 'locked together in seemingly endless male power struggles'.[17] *Europe* is remarkable for its vision both of contemporary Europe and of generic Christian history, and meshes the present moment of the French Revolution with the eighteen-hundred-year duration of the Christian epoch, seeing the two as radically continuous with each other. In this way, *Europe* is as much about the traditions and ideologies of the Christian tradition that the French Revolution challenges as it is about the specificities of contemporary events; it is about the nightmare of a conflictual and repressive Christian history and the hoped for apocalyptic awakening from that history.

The frontispiece to *Europe* (*IB* 156; *CIB* 174: see cover design to this volume) is one of Blake's most powerful and well-known designs – it is generally known as the 'Ancient of Days', though was not named so by Blake. In the design a white-haired, bearded, muscular figure leans out of a red, sun-like sphere to circumscribe an immense circle on the black void below with a pair of golden compasses. The plate, it seems, envisions the creation of the universe by the Christian deity, and echoes lines both from the Bible – 'When . . . he set a compass on the face of the depth' (Proverbs 8:27) – and John Milton's *Paradise Lost* (1674): 'in his hand/ He took the golden Compasses . . ./ . . . to circumscribe/ This Universe, and all created things' (Bk 7, ll. 224–7). The image, however, is of Blake's 'Urizen': his god of repression, circumscription and containment who, it is implied by the choice of frontispiece, is the presiding deity of both Christian and – in the shape of rational Deism – Enlightenment 'Europe'. Urizen, for Blake, is the ruling ideologue and demigod of European society, culture and politics at the end of the eighteenth century; he is the god who aspires, in the poem's words, to 'bind the infinite with an eternal band' (*CPP* 61; *CP* 227).

The dominant actors in *Europe*'s narrative are, however, the queen or goddess 'Enitharmon' and her consort 'Los'. They are figures of the contemporary ruling monarchical and ecclesiastical establishment, and are therefore the baleful operators of Urizenic ideology. Although female, Enitharmon is the historical mouthpiece of an unambiguously *patriarchal* political and religious ideology: an ideology that, as she presides over Christian history, she reproduces in a theology and morality of sin and punishment. Enitharmon declares her creed in a recognizable injunction to Christian moral prohibition, a dogma that has its political analogue in an ideology of passive acceptance that, surrendering 'Joy' in the historical present, fixes its hope miserably on the 'Eternal life [that] awaits the worms of sixty winters' – a heaven beyond the grave. Enitharmon calls on her kingly and priestly 'sons' thus:

> Arise O Rintrah thee I call! & Palamabron thee!
> Go! Tell the Human race that Womans love is Sin!
> That an Eternal life awaits the worms of sixty winters
> In an allegorical abode where existence hath never come:
> Forbid all Joy, & from her childhood shall the little female
> Spread nets in every secret path.
>
> My weary eyelids draw towards the evening, my bliss is yet but new.
>
> (*CPP* 62; *CP* 229)

'Go! Tell the Human race that Womans love is Sin', says Enitharmon; and, ideologically, her creed of guilt and punishment operates on several levels at once. In one sense, it is a psychology and morality of sin that instils self-abnegation and ascetic denial in the 'Human race' – with the result that demands for pleasure or 'Joy' are given up, and happiness or fulfilment deferred from social or earthly life to a spiritual, metaphysical and heavenly afterlife. The outcome of this doctrine is political passivity; it is the social and sexual outworking of the 'sacred code' that, as *The Marriage* puts it, says 'Evil. is alone from the Body' and 'Good. is alone from the Soul', the creed that threatens 'God will torment Man in Eternity for following his Energies' (*CPP* 34; *CP* 181). But Enitharmon's code has a significance in terms of sexual politics and gender ideology, too. Enitharmon announces that 'Womans love is Sin' so that 'Woman, lovely Woman! May have dominion' (*CPP* 62; *CP* 229); she constructs an ideology that ascribes woman's power or 'dominion' to sexuality and the body – to the arts, wiles and 'nets' of womanly sexual refusal and entrapment. She generates a religion built on the opposing poles of sexual chastity and 'sinful' seduction; but this supposed 'dominion' of woman is in fact *no* dominion at all, but rather the *subjection* of woman to the contradictory patriarchal ideology that defines her as either chaste virgin or polluted whore. It is the ethic of sexual purity/impurity that is forced so violently on (and exposed so painfully by) Oothoon in *Visions of the Daughters of Albion* (1793) – and it is also the derogative sexualization of women's power and bodies that is critiqued so fiercely by Mary Wollstonecraft in *Vindication of the Rights of Woman* (1792).[18]

But if Enitharmon's religion envelops the love and body of woman in 'sin' – denying woman and man the innocence of desire (as Oothoon is denied it) – Enitharmon does not forbid *herself* such 'bliss' or pleasure. In fact, she is a queen of pleasure, as is her kingly consort, Los. In the narrative of *Europe*, Enitharmon and Los inhabit what Blake calls a 'crystal house' (*CPP* 61, *CP* 228; *CPP* 65, *CP* 234) where they 'joy [. . .] in the peaceful night', 'drink the sparkling wine of Los', 'laugh at war', and 'Despis[e] toil and care,/ Because the days and nights of joy, in lucky hours renew' (*CPP* 62; *CP* 228). Blake presents the life of Enitharmon and Los as one of complacent luxury in a 'crystal house' that, strikingly, resembles nothing so much as a royal palace or mansion where an endless aristocratic party is conducted through history by the oblivious possessors of wealth and power. Seen in this context, Enitharmon and Los comprise a historical vision of aristocratic power and pleasure – robbing others of joy in their self-satisfied revelry, they suggest a picture of France's *ancien régime* nobility before the eruption of the Revolution. Los declares:

> The shrill winds wake!
> Till all the sons of Urizen look out and envy Los:
> Seize all the spirits of life and bind
> Their warbling joys to our loud strings
> Bind all the nourishing sweets of earth
> *To give us bliss . . .*
>
> (*CPP* 62; *CP* 228: my emphasis)

As well as a vision of French and European aristocracy in pre-revolutionary Europe, Enitharmon's and Los's rule is also a vision of Christian history – to the extent that, as we saw, state Christianity (the pernicious collusion of 'The King & the Priest' (*CPP* 473; *CP* 151)) undergirds social oppression. As an account of the reign and rule of state Christianity, *Europe*'s narrative covers the 'Eighteen hundred years' (*CPP* 63; *CP* 229) of historical Christendom – beginning with an allusion, at the start of the narrative, to Christ's birth in John Milton's 'On the Morning of Christ's Nativity' (1645). Milton's 'Heav'n-born child' (l.30) becomes Blake's messianic 'secret child' who descends 'thro' the orient gates of the eternal day' (*CPP* 61; *CP* 227); but the supposedly liberatory dawn of Christianity becomes the beginning of a reign of power as official Christianity catastrophically usurps spiritual vision – in the same way 'Priesthood' co-opted the expansive visions of poets into repressive creeds in *The Marriage of Heaven and Hell*. The false dawn of the Christian era in Blake's historical myth is succeeded by eighteen hundred years of oppressive history in which Enitharmon 'sleeps' and 'dreams' (*CPP* 63; *CP* 229–30) into existence her power, privilege and pleasure under the banner of Urizenic ideology; and for Blake Enitharmon's dream of royal or aristocratic wish-fulfilment *is Christian history* itself. At the end of eighteen hundred years, Enitharmon wakes in response to the 'howl thro Europe' (*CPP* 64; *CP* 233) of the terrifying revolutionary 'flames of Orc' (*CPP* 64; *CP* 232), and her historical supremacy begins to shatter. In a narrative reference to the American war, Blake envisions 'immortal demons of futurity' convulsing the established powers of the European continent, and 'Divid[ing] the heavens of Europe' (*CPP* 63; *CP* 230) in auguries of change.

But even after Enitharmon wakes from her dream of power, she continues to 'call [. . .] her sons & daughters/ To the sports of night,/ Within her crystal house' (*CPP* 65; *CP* 234), oblivious to all omens of historical transformation. As she calls, however, she finds her children – her progeny and subjects – are beginning to break free from her rule, to exceed her ideological regimen. She calls on 'Oothoon' in the following terms:

> I hear the soft Oothoon in Enitharmons tents:
> Why wilt thou give up womans secrecy my melancholy child?
> Between two moments bliss is ripe:
> O Theotormon robb'd of joy, I see thy salt tears flow
> Down the steps of my crystal house.
>
> (*CPP* 66; *CP* 235)

Lamenting Theotormon's misery with false regret – her *mission* is to rob her children of 'joy' – she anxiously importunes Oothoon not to give up 'womans secrecy'; that is, the contradictory patriarchal code that idealizes female chastity and demonizes 'Woman's love', and that Oothoon herself so passionately challenges in *Visions of the Daughters of Albion*. In *Europe* Oothoon – a revolutionary voice even if, as we saw in chapter 2, a repressed one – is evidently starting to challenge Enitharmon's Urizenic ideology, to contest its repressive terms. Enitharmon urges Orc, too, not to disturb but to augment the 'enormous revelry' of her regime:

> Orc! smile upon my children!
> Smile son of my afflictions.
> Arise O Orc and give our mountains joy of thy red light.
>
> (*CPP* 66; *CP* 235)

But in the poem's mythic narrative Orc's 'rising' is in tune with the break of revolutionary 'morning', not Enitharmon's aristocratic historical fantasy – and Enitharmon's waking to the revolutionary dawn after her long night of revelry brings an unwilling recognition that her subjects are out of her control, and that the tide of history has turned violently against her. Orc's 'light' will not warm or illuminate her 'crystal house' or pleasures any longer, for 'in the vineyards of red France appear'd the light of [Orc's] fury . . . And Enitharmon groan[ed] & crie[d] in anguish and dismay'.

Produced in 1794 – the year after the French king and queen were executed and in the period that the anti-counter-revolutionary Reign of Terror convulsed Europe (from September 1793 to mid 1794) – Blake's *Europe: A Prophecy* meditates the collapse of the French *ancien régime* in the 'red wheels dropping with blood' of revolutionary violence, a time when 'Tigers couch upon the prey & suck the ruddy tide' (*CPP* 66; *CP* 236). According to David Erdman, *Europe* also, in its closing narrative sections (see *CPP* 63–5; *CP* 230–34), invokes the 'English crusade of 1793–1794',[19] following Britain's declaration of war against France in 1793 – and the 'strife of blood' (*CPP* 66; *CP* 236) with which the poem ends promises an ongoing struggle. Blake's next prophetic poems, of 1794 and 1795, interrogate more and more the ideological terrors and torments of this revolutionary historical process, and struggle to find within it a prophetic vision of change.

4

Bibles of Hell: *The Song of Los, The [First] Book of Urizen, The Book of Los, The Book of Ahania*

The Song of Los (1795), as its punning title hints, is a song of 'loss'.

On the world-historical stage that Blake's myth increasingly occupies in the 1790s, the *Song* charts the decline or loss of emancipatory political and poetic vision in repressive ideological forms. The poem is a history and survey of world-historical mind that, symbolically, completes the visions of historical change given in the 'continental' prophecies, *America* and *Europe*. For the poem's two sections are titled 'AFRICA' (*CPP* 67–8; *CP* 237–9) and 'ASIA' (*CPP* 68–70; *CP* 239–41), and trace the dominance of Urizenic ideology in its religious and political manifestations on these continents. As in *Europe*, Urizenic dominance is secured through the imposition of imaginatively and politically constraining philosophies and creeds. However, the *Song* also anticipates the prospects of world-historical revolutionary transformation as the 'howl ris[ing] up from Europe' from Orc's rebel activity shakes the 'Kings of Asia' (*CPP* 68; *CP* 239) with fear. A song of 'loss' on one level, then, the poem is also the song of 'Los', Blake's 'Eternal Prophet' (*CPP* 67; *CP* 237), on another: a prophetic song that, like Los himself, preserves the vision of spiritual and social liberty in the midst of its historical loss and attenuation.

In *Europe*, Los is a compromised figure, the consort of the repressive and queenly Enitharmon; he belongs to the ruling ideological establishment. In *The Song of Los*, Los is again entangled in a fallen history, for the poem's inclusive narrative begins by showing 'Adam' and 'Noah' (the two biblical progenitors of new worlds) observing that 'Urizen g[a]ve his Laws to the Nations/ By the hands of the children of Los' (*CPP* 67; *CP* 237). Poetry and prophecy have, it seems, both been co-opted into the ruling or establishment ideology; poets have degenerated into priests who are operators of conservative thinking. At the back of this tale of 'loss' is the conversion of the works of imaginative 'poets' and artists into religious dogma, as outlined in *The Marriage of Heaven and Hell*: the congealing of 'poetic tales' into 'forms of worship' (*CPP* 38; *CP* 186), the loss of vision to law, and the 'appropriation of poetry by . . . priesthood'.[1] This double sense of potential *and* loss in *The Song of Los* gives the poem its ambivalent tone of lament and prophecy, for it is poised between the poles of mourning and affirmation. The designs that front and conclude the poem enact this ambivalence, for the frontispiece displays an abject worshipper kneeling before a dark hieroglyphic sun in an attitude of Urizenic subjection (*IB* 174; *CIB* 194), while the tailpiece shows Los as a smiling sun god – albeit a melancholic one – hovering over a burning orb whose fire he has apparently fashioned into artistic form (*IB* 181; *CIB* 201). The mournful aspect of Los's smile reminds us that Los – whose name punningly inverts the Latin 'Sol' for sun, the latter linking him to Apollo, the Greek god of poetry and the sun – is perpetually haunted by intimations of loss and fall. Los is an ambivalent narrative metaphor for the obliteration and potential restitution of political and imaginative liberty.

The Song of Los ends with the resonant line, 'Urizen Wept' (*CPP* 70; *CP* 241). This is Urizen's response to Orc's fires 'raging in European darkness', but also to the failure of his formerly unassailable reign; for, as he floats over the 'heavens/ Of Europe', Urizen's 'Books of brass iron & gold' begin to 'Melt' (*CPP* 69; *CP* 240). Urizen's weeping echoes the shortest verse in the Bible, 'Jesus wept' (John 11:35), which narrates Jesus's mourning over the death of Lazarus; and just as Jesus's act prefaces Lazarus's raising from the dead, so Blake's poem prophesies the raising of nations and continents from Urizen's deadly dominance.

The *Song* anticipates Urizen's overthrow, but does so only at the level of desire; for the poem remains darkened by the non-fulfilment of the world-historical transformations for which it longs. Indeed, the tone of Blake's mid-1790s prophecies to which we now turn – *The [First] Book of Urizen* (1794), *The Book of Los* (1795) and *The Book of Ahania* (1795) – is predominantly one of lament, for these works find, even in the revolutionary historical convulsions they meditate, the reanimation of political repression alongside transformative revolution. *The [First] Book of Urizen*, for instance, is a complex and traumatized work which narrates a struggle for power in the heavens and history, but that renders the *meaning* of the revolutionary historical changes that it contemplates indeterminate. Like Orc's tumultuous eruption in *America* and *Europe*, Urizen's darkly cataclysmic activity in *The [First] Book of Urizen* is depicted in the language of the sublime. But just as Orc's historical rising emerges as a 'sublime' question mark, so Urizen's energies are shrouded in uncertainty. Here is the description of Urizen's rise to power in Eternity at the beginning of Blake's poem:

> 1. Lo, a shadow of horror is risen
> In Eternity! Unknown, unprolific!
> Self-closed, all-repelling: what Demon
> Hath form'd this abominable void
> This soul-shudd'ring vacuum? – Some said
> 'It is Urizen', But unknown, abstracted
> Brooding secret, the dark power hid.
>
> (*CPP* 70; *CP* 242)

'Shadow', 'Unknown', 'closed', 'repelling', 'void', 'vacuum', 'abstracted', 'secret', 'dark', 'hid': these relentless negatives suggest that Urizen's rising is an unknown trauma, catastrophe or convulsion deranging Eternity's ability to identify or interpret it. It is arguable, in fact, that the emergence of Urizen in *The [First] Book of Urizen* is *itself a trauma*: for Blake's presentation of Urizen's rising in Eternity involves images both of 'revolutionary' insurrection and 'reactionary' tyranny, and Urizen himself is a historically ambivalent or contradictory figure who signifies both archaic religious and political authority *and* revolutionary or 'Enlightenment' secularism. Urizen in *The [First] Book of Urizen*, that is to say, is a traumatic or 'sublime' sign of the radical indeterminacy and, in a sense, *unreadability* of the history that Blake is addressing in the mid 1790s. Tilottama Rajan comments:

> Writing in the 1790s, Blake does not have the apocalyptic privilege of disengaging himself from events, both past and present. As is suggested by the tormented family romances that traverse these [1790s] texts, history is the scene of the [Blakean] system's psychoanalysis, an unconscious or radical alterity inseparable from its prehistory in trauma.[2]

The 'trauma' to which Rajan refers is what she calls the 'unmanageability [. . .] of history'[3] in the 1790s; and this unmanageability, for Blake as well as other English radicals of the period, is the traumatic inversion of jubilant political liberation in France at the beginning of the decade into the nightmare of the anti-counter-revolutionary Reign of Terror in the mid 1790s. The year in which *The [First] Book of Urizen* was produced – 1794 – was the year that saw the culmination of the Terror under Maximilien de Robespierre. In the Great Terror of June and July of that year, for instance, more counter-revolutionists (1,376) were guillotined in Paris in forty-nine days than had been executed in the entire fifteen months previously. The violence of the revolutionary Terror is mythologized by Blake in *The Book of Ahania* (1795), as we will see, but *Urizen* is a book that strives to diagnose the *ideological* terrors underpinning the disastrous 'Urizenic' degeneration of revolution into political repression.

As well as punning on the idea of the bound or 'horizon' (see below), Urizen's name is a pun that suggests *your-reason*: and thus Urizen ironizes the universally privileged category of Enlightenment thinking, 'Reason', as well as the work of the pre-revolutionary *philosophes*, Voltaire and Rousseau, whose thought contributed to the ferment of rational critique that culminated in the French Revolution. More directly, Urizen's double status as both god of transcendent law and god of Reason relates him to movements by the French National Convention in the revolutionary decade to replace traditional Catholicism with a new, secular, 'rational' religion. In late 1793, for instance, a bizarre ceremony was held in Paris that renamed the cathedral of Notre Dame the 'Temple of Reason'. But only six months later Reason was deposed from her new position by Robespierre himself, a deist who despised atheism; and in June 1794 Robespierre presided over a festival of the Supreme Being, enthroning an abstract deistic divinity in both God's and Reason's place. Urizen's election of himself in *The [First] Book of*

Urizen as the supreme god of an abstract law – announcing his creed as that of 'One command, one joy, one desire,/ One curse, one weight, one measure/ One King, one God, one Law' (*CPP* 72; *CP* 245) – parodies these revolutionary, secularizing attempts to invent alternative myths of rational (and political) transcendence. Indeed, Blake's poem sees such attempts as the *repetition* rather than revision of traditional metaphysical errors – and sees them, moreover, as the ideological foundation of political coercion and political 'terror'.

For radical artists like Blake, the tragedy of the mid 1790s is the disastrous reversal of political liberation into repression – the reversion of revolution to tyranny when rebellion repeats rather than revises the thing that it opposes. In the figure of Urizen, indeed, revolution and repression echo one another – for Urizen is a symbol both of the traditional metaphysical authority of God, priest and king, *and* of the usurping 'Enlightenment' authority of Reason. It is this ambivalence that produces the indeterminacy of the political meanings of *The [First] Book of Urizen*; and that makes it possible, as Robert Essick points out, to read the poem's bitter excoriation of Urizen's ideology of 'One King, one God, one Law' as both a satire on George III, Anglicanism and the unwritten constitution of England, *and* on Maximilien de Robespierre, the cult of the Supreme Being and the written constitution of France that was at the time being forged by the National Assembly.[4] *Urizen* is a poem, then, that participates in and in a certain way *repeats* the traumas of revolutionary political struggle in the mid 1790s – repeats them, that is, in the anxious indeterminacies of its own political signification.

As well as an oblique reflection on the contemporary revolutionary historical process, *The [First] Book of Urizen* is a radical text that assaults the strongholds of cultural authority in late eighteenth-century Britain. Like *The Marriage of Heaven and Hell*, it commits itself to overturning the 'Bibles or sacred codes' (*CPP* 34; *CP* 181) of established cultural tradition. Strikingly and scandalously, it is a rewriting of the first book of the pre-eminent text of authority in late eighteenth-century European culture: the Bible. Just as Genesis is 'The First Book of Moses' in the Bible, Blake's parody of the Mosaic myth of origins is titled 'The [*First*] Book of Urizen'; it is a book in Blake's 'Bible of Hell' (*CPP* 44;

CP 194). Parodying the textual form of the King James – or 'Authorized' – version of the Bible by being divided into numbered 'chapters' and 'verses' and double columns of text, *Urizen* desacralizes and debunks the supposed authority of the Bible to give the 'authorized' or *ur*-version of humankind's spiritual history. Like *The Marriage, The [First] Book of Urizen* audaciously rewrites the sacred. Although, like Genesis, a book about the 'Fall' of humankind – the tale of Urizen's fall, indeed, comes in 'CHAP: III' (see *CPP* 72–4, *CP* 245–7) of the poem as Genesis's account of Adam and Eve's fall is given in chapter 3 of that book – *Urizen* scandalously attributes humanity's Fall to the *errors* of orthodoxy, rather than the challenge to it. A simultaneously parodic and tormented work, *Urizen* is about the *catastrophe* of orthodoxy insofar as orthodoxy imposes limitation and constriction upon the expansive possibilities of vision, imagination and desire – what Blake calls the 'all flexible senses' of the 'Immortal' (*CPP* 71; *CPP* 243) – that pertained in the prelapsarian condition occupied by the 'Eternals' before Urizen's cataclysmic rising.

The tyrannous God of Reason, Urizen is also Blake's version of the patriarchal God of Judaeo-Christian religion: the transcendent, holy, unimpeachable deity of creation, law and judgement who rules 'From the depths of dark solitude . . ./ The eternal abode in my holiness,/ Hidden set apart in my stern counsels/ Reserv'd for the days of futurity' (*CPP* 71; *CP* 244). For Blake, Urizen is an abstract, mysterious and autocratic lawgiver whose created world is a fearful metaphor for the oppressive creeds and punishing laws of the Church and the State. By heretically rewriting the sacred text of the Bible in an alternative satirical myth of cosmological origins, *The [First] Book of Urizen* participates in that movement of Enlightened, sceptical critique at the end of the eighteenth century that, in Jon Mee's words, saw the Bible as 'the ultimate sacred text of the state', and an 'essential . . . part of the hegemony of the ruling classes': a critique that contended the Bible 'needed to be read as a poetic document in the light of the reader's active judgement rather than a rigid, sacred authority'.[5] This is what Blake's *The [First] Book of Urizen* performs: for it reimagines the sacred text in a critical and satirical version relevant to its own historical moment – just as, in *The Marriage*, Isaiah and Ezekiel become prophets of spiritual and political contemporaneity.

A figure of political and religious constraint, Urizen is the demigod of the 'boundary': his activity is to set 'bounds' round energy and imagination, and his name transliterates the Greek *ourizein*, meaning 'horizon', or to 'mark out by boundaries, lay down, mark out: to limit, define'.[6] Declaring his paranoid desire for mastery over the world and the other Eternals, Urizen boasts:

> 5 First I fought with the fire; consum'd
> Inwards, into a deep world within:
> A void immense, wild dark & deep,
> Where nothing was; Natures wide womb
> And self balanc'd stretch'd o'er the void
> I alone, even I! the winds merciless
> Bound; but condensing, in torrents
> They fall & fall; strong I repell'd
> The vast waves, & arose on the waters
> A wide world of solid obstruction
>
> (*CPP* 72; *CP* 244)

'Self balanc'd . . ./ I alone, even I!': Urizen's language here reveals that his binding activity is an assertion of his will and ego, a bid for power that is the imposition of his limited narcissistic vision on others. A slave to the law of 'Reason', Urizen disastrously imposes this law on everyone, materializing *The Marriage*'s dictum that 'One Law for the Lion & Ox is Oppression' (*CPP* 44; *CP* 194). Urizen's *Book* mimes the constrictions that his anxious activities institute, for the designs in the poem depict bodies imprisoned, writhing, howling and falling in attitudes of terrible incarceration, gripped by the apparently inescapable limitation of their 'Eternal' being within Urizen's 'world of solid obstruction'. A vision of the dominance of constrictive, reactionary Urizenic ideology, the verbal text of *Urizen*, too, mimics the containments that it dramatizes: arranged in cramped, numbered columns that mock the form of the printed biblical text yet remain (literally) contained by it, the poem is 'made to suit the moment when poetry congeals into scripture', as Edward Larrissy says. He adds: 'The verse is infected with the limitations of the Fall it describes: its appearance on the page is that of poetry congealing into scripture'.[7] A book about Urizen, the poem is also the 'Book *of* Urizen' insofar as it reproduces the irresistible terrors of Urizen's ideological hegemony, visiting 'dark visions of torment' (*CPP* 70; *CP* 242) on its protagonists, readers and viewers.

In visual terms, images of anguished struggle against Urizen's tyrannical edicts dominate the poem. On Plate 6 (of copy G), for instance, Los is depicted in a terrifying image of silent or speechless howling (see *IB* 189; *CIB* 208). His constrained and foreshortened form crouches beneath darkened flames; he clutches his head in violent anguish, and his mouth is wide open in a tongueless and toothless keen of torment. David Worrall, seeing this image as a representation of the plight of radical political vision and dissent in William Pitt's reactionary Britain of the mid 1790s, comments: 'The anti-sedition campaigns of the early 1790s have made this man silent. The visual grammar of manacled men with padlocked lips . . . was . . . thoroughly absorbed into popular culture by [the mid 1790s]'.[8] Indeed, as well as a parody – as we saw above – of the prohibitive ideology of 'Reason' promulgated by the French National Convention in the 1790s, *Urizen* darkly satirizes the years 'described by contemporaries as "Pitt's Terror"' in Britain. These were years characterized, says Worrall, 'by political trauma because London was an imperial centre frightened by fears of invasion by France without and by reform within . . . In 1794, the first full year of war [between Britain and France], the winter began with sensational treason trials which indicted radical activists drawn from the very London liberal intelligentsia which was on the edges of Blake's personal circle of acquaintance'.[9] In *The [First] Book of Urizen*, the plight of the radical artist in Pitt's Britain is allegorized in part by Los's catastrophic 'rent' (*CPP* 74; *CP* 246) from Urizen's side through the latter's disastrous fall from Eternity; for the anguished division of the artist's visionary energy from a new and virulently repressive regime of statecraft and priestcraft leaves the artist 'lost' in a chaos of division and conflict to which he is powerlessly subjected, and to which he can find no adequate response. Los in *Urizen* is indeed in a position of loss, for he is 'affrighted/ At the formless unmeasurable death' (*CPP* 74; *CP* 247) of the ruinous world that Urizen's arrogation of power has brought about, and he spends the poem struggling to stem and staunch the traumatic and conflictual chaos of Urizen's reign. Paradoxically, by attempting imperiously to impose law, rule and boundary upon the fluid and flexible life of 'Eternity', Urizen has unwittingly fragmented and disorganized the very social body that he wishes to bind into law and unity. 'Los', then, becomes the prophet left with the task of fashioning a redemptive vision out of the rifted and ruined remains of Urizen's disastrous creation; and on this level Los images Blake as a radical artist struggling to find an emancipatory and regenerative vision within a situation of political repression. Like Los, however, Blake as a radical artist is forced to work in a situation of irreducible and irreparable reduction, subordinated to the hegemony of Urizenic rule at the same time as he resists its hubris.

Los's plight in *The [First] Book of Urizen* is simultaneously political and religious. The victory of Urizenic ideology in the poem means that Los is hopelessly disempowered in Urizen's botched and fractured world. Although Urizen's dream of a 'solid without fluctuation' (*CPP* 71; *CP* 244) and of 'one King, one God, one Law' (*CPP* 72; *CP* 245) tumbles into chaos in the poem – and Los spends his time struggling to rebuild a vision of prophetic form from within Urizen's 'ruinous fragments of life' (*CPP* 73; *CP* 245) – Los is unable to redeem the deathly forms of Urizen's world. Instead, Los remains subjected to the baneful consequences of Urizen's constrictive creations, subordinated to the ascendancy of Urizenic ideology. Blake's poem allegorizes this dilemma by showing how Los abjectly *repeats* Urizen's divisive 'binding' of the world to his desire, for Los's 'loss' is the traumatic collapse of any available or viable alternatives to Urizen's merciless universe.

All Los can do in response to Urizen's fragmentation of the flexible, fraternal social body of Eternity is to 'bind' Urizen's fissured and fallen body all over again – in an effort to save him from unredeemable formlessness. Any redemptive binding that Los achieves, however, is irreparably compromised by the depredations of Urizen's 'vast world' (*CPP* 73; *CP* 246); and Los wretchedly rehearses Urizen's atomizing collapse. Just as Urizen's binding of the 'winds' fails when they 'condense' and 'in torrents . . . fall & fall' (*CPP* 72; *CP* 244) in 'CHAP: II' of the poem, Los's binding of Urizen's chaotic body fails:

1: In terrors Los shrunk from his task:
His great hammer fell from his hand:
His fires beheld, and sickening,
Hid their strong limbs in smoke.
For with noises ruinous loud;
With hurtlings & clashings & groans
The Immortal endur'd his chains,
Tho' bound in a deadly sleep.

(*CPP* 77; *CP* 250)

Los's hammer wanes, and Urizen's spoliations repeat themselves in Los's labours. For though the bindings of prophetic art seek to staunch the divisions and disruptions of Urizen's repressive forms, they end up repeating the disasters they deny, and each act of artistic binding becomes another act of division.

This structure of binding-and-division is repeated throughout *The [First] Book of Urizen* like a trauma compulsively revisited. Urizen separates himself from Eternity and strives to fix himself in the unity of 'one Law' (*CPP* 72; *CP* 245), but falls; Los, frightened at Urizen's 'hurtling bones' (*CPP* 74; *CP* 247), binds him, but is then 'divided' (*CPP* 78; *CP* 251) into masculine and feminine forms; the Eternals build a tent round Los and his female form, 'Enitharmon', to 'bind in the Void' (*CPP* 78; *CP* 252), but 'shudder' when they see Los 'begetting his likeness,/ On his own divided image' (*CPP* 79; *CP* 253); 'Orc', the issue of this coupling, threatens Los in Oedipal challenge and Los 'chain[s] his young limbs to [a] rock' (*CPP* 79; *CP* 254); Los is himself bound by a 'Chain of Jealousy' that forms in the day and is 'burst in twain' (*CPP* 80; *CP* 254) at night; Urizen observes that 'no flesh nor spirit could keep/ His iron laws one moment' (*CPP* 81; *CP* 256), and as he wanders above his cities the 'Net of Religion' (*CPP* 82; *CP* 257) forms behind him, 'dividing' (*CPP* 82; *CP* 256) the heavens; the inhabitants of Urizen's cities become 'bound down/ To earth by their narrowing perceptions' (*CPP* 83; *CP* 257), but one of his sons, 'Fuzon', 'call[s] together' his brothers and sisters, and they name Urizen's world 'Egypt, & le[ave] it' (*CPP* 83; *CP* 258). In this succession of bindings and unbindings, Los's desire for artistic form is inescapably imbricated with Urizen's repressive constrictions, and the struggle for liberty is entwined with the fall into chaos, for the poem is unable to separate Los's regenerative labours from the ruinations produced by Urizen.

Earlier, we noted that the *trauma* of Urizen's rising in *The [First] Book of Urizen* points to the historical confusion in the mid 1790s between revolution and reaction, insurgency and tyranny, rebellion and terror; for Urizen is a figure both of Enlightenment Reason and traditional religion, and compounds these meanings troublingly with one another. And it is arguable that, in a certain way, Los in *The [First] Book of Urizen* repeats this Urizenic double bind, for his labours reproduce Urizen's authoritarian limitations even as he resists the demigod's terrors; both Los and Urizen are unsettlingly both revolutionists and recidivists. Los's remorseless rebuilding or 'binding' of the shattered body of Urizen in the poem is, in many ways, Blake's allegory of a progressivist or revolutionary attempt to build a new social world or body out of the ruins of the old order. Thus David Worrall says that Los's building of 'time' in the poem – when he forges 'chains new & new/ Numb'ring with links. hours, days & years' (*CPP* 75; *CP* 248) – has 'parallels with the introduction of a French revolutionary calendar in 1793 to replace the Gregorian version'.[10] The Revolution strove to make the world new, but the anxiety of Blake's mid 1790s poems is that its energies collapse miserably into the repetition of the old: a forging of 'chains new'.

At the end of *Urizen*, as we saw, one of Urizen's sons, Fuzon, gathers his siblings together and leaves Urizen's world – which he names 'Egypt' (*CPP* 83; *CP* 258). This conclusion opens immediately on to the narrative of Blake's next poem, *The Book of Ahania* (1795), which, just as *Urizen* is his hellish version of Genesis, is Blake's diabolical rewriting of the biblical book of Exodus. The Bible's Exodus tells the story of Old Testament Israel's liberation from slavery in Egypt under Moses' leadership, and its journey to Canaan, the promised land of freedom. 'Fuzon', in this connection, is a liberatory Moses figure to Urizen's tyrannical Pharaoh; but Fuzon and Urizen are also mythological analogues of other antagonistic pairings in literary and religious tradition. Fuzon is an insurgent who defies Urizen's rule, and as such is an analogue of Christ as a liberator from the regime of law and punishment superintended by the patriarchal, Old Testament God. In Blake's narrative, though, Fuzon ends up as a defeated Christ crushed by Urizen's tyranny, 'nail'd' unregeneratingly to the 'Tree of MYSTERY' (*CPP* 87; *CP* 263). In another sense, Fuzon as rebel is associated with the

Bible's and Milton's Satan: the fierce yet flawed defier of God's unanswerable regimen. Fuzon's fieriness also links him to the classical Prometheus, the heroic rebel who filched fire from the gods for humankind, but was defeated by the patriarchal Jupiter. The common thread in these narratives is the wretched defeat of a potentially successful revolution: even Moses, who, Blake's narrative implies, begins as a liberator, ends up ideologically absorbed into the law as, in Exodus, he delivers God's stern decalogue from Mount Sinai (see the book of Exodus, chapter 20). In *Ahania*, in fact, the rock that slaughters Fuzon falls on the earth and becomes 'Mount Sinai, in Arabia' (*CPP* 86; *CP* 262).

There is another, contemporary historical analogue for Fuzon's brief rebel career and precipitate defeat: the fate of Maximilien de Robespierre, the idealistic architect of the anti-counter-revolutionary Terror who, in July 1794 (the year before *Ahania*), was executed by his own favoured engine of political violence and vengeance, the guillotine. Fuzon begins his revolution by mocking Urizen in a jibe aimed both at the god of abstract 'Reason' (the French National Convention's goddess of Reason was deposed, of course, by Robespierre in June 1794) and at the Catholic, Judaeo-Christian god of 'Mystery' (Robespierre was closely associated with the campaign to de-Christianize the French revolutionary republic in the early 1790s):

> 2: Shall we worship this Demon of smoke,
> Said Fuzon, this abstract non-entity
> This cloudy God seated on waters
> Now seen, now obscured, King of sorrow?
>
> (*CPP* 84; *CP* 259)

Fuzon materializes his sacrilegious insult against Urizen by assaulting him with a 'vast globe' of moulded fire, a literalization of his repressed rebel desire. Once hurled, Fuzon's globe flies 'burning' and 'Length[ens] into a hungry beam' (*CPP* 84; *CP* 259); and David Erdman suggests that Fuzon's weapon is 'an anthropomorphic guillotine'.[11] Fuzon's 'exulting flam'd beam' (*CPP* 84; *CP* 259) fails to defeat Urizen, however, and in the war in heaven that follows between them, Urizen triumphs. The grim design that concludes *Ahania* (see *IB* 213; *CIB* 237) offers an image of the concrete results of Urizen's and Fuzon's struggle and Fuzon's defeat, and is recognized by Blake's commentators as unusual in its degree of 'close realism':[12] Erdman proposes that it is a 'heap of the fruit of guillotine'.[13] The design clearly depicts a severed head to the top right, blood falling from its sliced neck; underneath and adjacent to the head are fleshy, naked body parts – limbs, perhaps a torso, perhaps buttocks[14] – and below and to the left, a woman's (apparently unsevered) head with red hair. Further to the left is another mop of brown hair, the crown of the head to the fore so that its likely decapitation is obscured. This dark and gruesome 'FINIS' – the last, tailpiece word of the poem (*CPP* 90; *CP* 266) – seems to present the final outcome of the violent struggle between Urizen and Fuzon. It is an image of both Fuzon's and Robespierre's ends, and also of the end of the attempt decisively to overthrow Urizen's ideological hegemony. For, miserably, Fuzon in the poem ends up *repeating* rather than replacing Urizen's cold hubristic terrors – in a more literal and desolate manner than even Los's echoing of Urizen in *The [First] Book of Urizen*.

In fact, Blake's mythologization of the historical process in the mid 1790s enacts a sublime of traumatic ambivalence in which revolution's historical epiphany is ever more perilously suspended between the poles of emergence and defeat, revelation and obliteration. In *The Book of Ahania*, as we have seen, Blake overlays his allegory of contemporary historical tumult on a Biblical typology in which the rebel Fuzon reprises Moses from the book of Exodus – but Fuzon, like Moses, declines from being a political emancipator to a petrifying lawgiver. Although these Biblical typologies belong to Blake's antinomian and millenarian language in the 1790s – where, as we saw in *America*, Biblical prophecy and history fuse – this language becomes increasingly muted in his mid-1790s 'Books': for these works are abjectly immersed in repetitions of lapsarian catastrophe, rather than revelations of contemporary apocalypse. In *The Book of Ahania*, indeed, Urizen and Fuzon traumatically *merge* with one another when they should, in apocalyptic terms, be opposites. The category of 'trauma' is relevant here because it suggests the abjectness of a certain *symbolic collapse* in Blake's mid-1790s works when he strives, dividedly, to narrativize the chaotic revolutionary process: for, in these works, reaction and revolt, repression and rebellion, liberty and tyranny become indistinguishable as unmanageable symptoms of historical ambiguity.

Arguably, such symbolic indeterminacies symptomatize the trauma of Europe's revolutionary history itself in the 1790s.

The Book of Ahania ties Urizen and Fuzon together from the start, as not just ideological antagonists, but mirror images. As father and son, they compete with each other Oedipally for supremacy in a complex and overdetermined narrative that is simultaneously historical allegory, religious parody and tormented psycho-sexual family romance. Early in the text, just as he is gathering his fiery strength to challenge Urizen, Fuzon is described as 'Son of Urizens silent burnings' (*CPP* 84; *CP* 259); and this echoing between the two figures suggests that Fuzon is an aspect of Urizen's *own* being. Fuzon is Urizen's 'son' and likeness. He is an externalization of Urizen's 'silent burnings', that is, his repressed desire or libidinal being – that aspect of Urizen's humanity that he is trying to deny, that he is rendering 'silent'. But Urizen's repressed libidinality cannot be conclusively erased, and its strangled energy returns viciously upon Urizen in the form of an enraged Fuzon – like the destructive return of the repressed in psychoanalytic theory. In response to Fuzon's fierce and fiery 'beam', Urizen uprears an icy 'broad Disk' (*CPP* 84; *CP* 259) in opposition, and the struggle between the two engines of war is described as follows:

> 5: [The Disk] was forg'd in mills where winter
> Beats incessant; ten winters the disk
> Unremitting endur'd the cold hammer.
>
> 6: But the strong arm that sent it, remember'd
> The sounding beam; laughing it tore through
> That beaten mass: keeping its direction
> The cold loins of Urizen dividing.
>
> (*CPP* 84; *CP* 260)

'The strong arm that sent it, *remember'd*/ The sounding beam': paradoxically, Urizen's icy opposition to Fuzon's 'sounding beam' 'remembers' or revivifies the very thing that it is attempting to deny. The repressed returns, and Fuzon's unquestionably phallic 'flam'd beam' (*CPP* 84; *CP* 259) divides Urizen's 'cold loins' in a castrating wound. The product of Fuzon's Oedipal assault against Urizen's repressed desire is the anguished (and ironic) spectacle of Urizen's smothered sexuality awakening in yet another externalized image, but this time a feminine one –

the figure of 'Ahania', who gives her name to the *Book*. Here is Ahania's origin in the moment of Urizen's sexual division:

> 7: Dire shriek'd his invisible Lust
> Deep groan'd Urizen! stretching his awful hand
> Ahania (so name his parted soul)
> He seiz'd on his mountains of Jealousy.
> He groand anguishd & called her Sin,
> Kissing her and weeping over her;
> Then hid her in darkness in silence;
> Jealous tho' she was invisible.
>
> (*CPP* 84–5; *CP* 260)

Patriarchally banishing Ahania – a figure of his own desire and femininity – from his self-deluding masculinity, Urizen's repudiation of his 'parted soul' turns Ahania into an image of everything that his grotesque phallicism subordinates. Ahania is a figure of all Urizen debars from his being; and his repression of her is the poem's mythic and ironic version of the *psycho-sexual* origins of conventional Judaeo-Christian religion. In Urizen's triumphant masculinist world, Ahania becomes a diminished and despised figure of 'Pestilence', a repository of 'Sin' and death and corruption whose exile echoes Oothoon's banishment by Bromion and Theotormon in *Visions of the Daughters of Albion*:

> 8: She fell down a faint shadow wandring
> In chaos and circling dark Urizen,
> As the moon anguishd circles the earth;
> Hopeless! abhorrd! a death-shadow,
> Unseen, unbodied, unknown,
> The mother of Pestilence.
>
> (*CPP* 85; *CP* 260)

This exile and marginalization of Ahania is the price that the Oedipal, masculine conflict between Urizen and Fuzon pays to maintain itself: their war of mutual male mirroring has a woman as its victim. In their violent, unbending, narcissistic agon of self-assertion, Urizen and Fuzon compete for the same patriarchal symbolic space; and their drama is a sacrificial dialectic in which, in mythological terms, twin male deities struggle for the place of transcendence, erasing woman from their vaunting self-promotion and banishing her to the margin of non-entity. Locked in an Oedipal struggle between father and son in which they become inseparable from one another, Urizen and Fuzon vie for pre-eminence, denying all dependency both on each other and on woman. Rebel and revolutionary though he is, Fuzon is a Urizen in waiting, and even proclaims himself that in a fleeting moment of their battle when, 'his tygers unloosing', he thinks 'Urizen slain by his wrath' and declares: 'I am God . . . eldest of things!' (*CPP* 86; *CP* 261).

At once a satire on the French revolutionary republic's creation of new 'gods' and on the claims of the Judaeo-Christian god to supremacy, Fuzon's 'Urizenic' boast is for Blake a simultaneously spiritual and political disaster; for it justifies a system of power erected on the basis of hierarchy and tyranny. It is the loss of liberty on every level. Strikingly, the dead-end of Urizen's and Fuzon's conflict in the poem offers no political ways forward at all: the *Book* leaves us, at the end, with a design filled with severed heads and limbs, a narrative with Fuzon 'groan[ing] on the Tree' (*CPP* 88; *CP* 264), and Urizenic ideology triumphant. The final chapter of *Ahania*, not really part of the narrative at all – but rather a mournful gloss on that narrative – leaves us with the voice of Ahania herself lamenting her exile and the death of liberty, love and joy that Urizen's and Fuzon's tyrannies have brought about. Her voice is heard 'lamenting' and 'Weeping upon the void'; like Oothoon, she exists 'on the verge/ Of Non-entity', and mourns round the 'Tree of Fuzon' and across the 'Abyss' that sunders her from Urizen (*CPP* 88; *CP* 264). Any 'prophecy' of future historical restitution is sunk in the lows of Ahania's beautiful visionary elegy – which is turned not towards futurity but to an irremediably lost past, when Urizen sowed the wisdom of 'eternal science' in the 'virgins of springing joy' (*CPP* 89; *CP* 266). The loss of Ahania's 'interchange sweet' (*CPP* 89; *CP* 265) with Urizen, however, leaves her with 'no form' (*CPP* 88; *CP* 264) in which to appear: she is like Oothoon without a body, and her exile (again like Oothoon's) is a metaphor for the banishment of all alternative political vision in Urizen's rocky world.

Ahania's song is a voice of historical exile; and Blake begins his next poem of the 1790s, *The Book of Los* (1795), with another lamenting female voice. This is the dirge of 'Eno aged Mother', who sits 'beneath the eternal Oak' and shakes the earth with an impassioned elegy for the 'Times remote!' when 'Love & Joy were adoration:/ And none impure were deem'd' (*CPP* 90; *CP* 267). As her language suggests, Eno mourns the loss of a vision or state of being that, she implies, existed prior to the ascendency of Urizenic law or state religion: before Urizen's 'sacred codes' (*The Marriage*: *CPP* 34; *CP* 181) tyrannously judged desire and joy to be 'sin', impurity, corruption. Like *The Song of Los*, *The Book of Los* is a book of 'loss'; but it is a still darker vision than the *Song*. Eno is depicted on the frontispiece of the *Book* (see *IB* 214; *CIB* 240) as a crouching and constricted figure beneath the eternal Oak; her knees are drawn up, her arms held in, and her mouth is opened in a hollow lament. Her attitude of crushing constraint echoes the abject sense of her speech, for the vision she opines is one that is irrevocably lost, and she speaks from a position of dispossession. The inaccessibility of the utopian state that she mourns is reinforced by the unreadable or elusive nature of her vision, for she celebrates a fluid movement between bounded contraries in which distinctions between opposites are radically suspended, and become sublimely indeterminate:

> 4: But Covet was poured full:
> Envy fed with fat of lambs:
> Wrath with lions gore:
> Wantonness lulld to sleep
> With the virgins lute,
> Or sated with her love.
>
> 5: Till Covet broke his locks & bars,
> And slept with open doors:
> Envy sung at the rich mans feast:
> Wrath was follow'd up and down
> By a little ewe lamb
> And Wantonness on his own true love
> Begot a giant race:
>
> (*CPP* 90–1; *CP* 267–8)

The contraries Eno marshals here lose their boundaries, and are opened up effortlessly to infinitude: they dissolve fluidly into each other. But Eno's elegy halts abruptly when she shifts into a narrative of Los's anguished struggles in Urizen's bounded world. The narrative following her elegy revisits the moment in *The [First] Book of Urizen* when Los's attempts to subdue Urizen lead to his being 'clos'd' with Urizen in a 'cold solitude & dark void' (*CPP* 77; *CP* 251). Despite the 'flames of desire' that rip furiously through heaven and earth, the narrative of *The Book of Los* introduces Los 'bound':

> 6: Raging furious the flames of desire
> Ran thro' heaven & earth, living flames
> Intelligent, organiz'd: arm'd
> With destruction & plagues. In the midst
> The Eternal Prophet bound in a chain
> Compell'd to watch Urizens shadow
>
> (*CPP* 91; *CP* 268)

As with the exiled Ahania in *The Book of Ahania*, who becomes a destructive 'Pestilence' (*CPP* 85; *CP* 260) in Urizen's world, Los's prophetic 'living flames' of desire turn malevolent and pestilential under Urizenic repression; and Los himself is subordinated to Urizen's supremacy. Despite his struggles, Los is incorporated in Urizen's repressive forms of spiritual, imaginative and political containment; his position is described thus:

> 10: Coldness, darkness, obstruction, a Solid
> Without fluctuation, hard as adamant
> Black as marble of Egypt; impenetrable
> Bound in the fierce raging Immortal.
> And the seperated fires froze in
> A vast solid without fluctuation,
> Bound in his clear expanding senses
>
> (*CPP* 91; *CP* 268–9)

Los's inability to 'bear/ The hard bondage' (*CPP* 92; *CP* 269) of what Jon Mee calls Urizen's 'system of state religion'[15] leads him, however, furiously to 'ren[d]' Urizen's 'vast solid . . . into numberless fragments' (*CPP* 92; *CP* 269) in a sublime gesture of Orcian and Fuzonic political revolt. Blake's focus in *The Book of Los*, though, is less on revolutionary *politics* – as it is *The Book of Ahania* – than on revolutionary *poetics*: that is to say, on how to fashion and preserve an artistic vision of liberty and infinitude within the cold constrictions of Urizen's ideological regime. In *The Book of Los*, in fact, liberatory poetic vision is in radical jeopardy; for, as in *The [First] Book of Urizen*, Los's activities seem to *reproduce* Urizen's creative catastrophes rather than transformatively reconfigure them. *The Book of Los,* then, mournfully stresses the *limitations* rather than liberations of Los's labour; indeed, his work in the poem is confined to the production of creative 'illusions' that obscure rather than liberate the visions of eternity. Jon Mee, therefore, suggests that *The Book of Los* is about the 'struggle between the prophet-bard and his rival the druid-priest':[16] a struggle, however, that (we might add) is enacted not just *between* Urizen and Los but also *within Los himself,* for Blake's Lambeth 'Books' indicate that the poet-prophet is always in danger of *becoming* the druid-priest, and the visionary artist a potential promulgator of ideological and establishment 'illusions'.

When Los, in parodic mimicry of the Urizenic God of Genesis, fashions 'infinite fires' into the 'immense Orb' (*CPP* 94; *CP* 271) of the sun, the sun is described as a 'glowing illusion' (*CPP* 94; *CP* 272) because it confines the infinity of fire in an orb-like form, limiting the vision of eternity to a sphere. David Worrall argues that Los's creation here invokes the notion of sun worship – that is, a 'symbolic religion based upon the natural world'[17] – but Urizen, of course, lies behind this metaphysical phantasm as its abstract, formless, unapproachable supremo. In fact, although Los seizes 'the vast Spine of Urizen' and 'b[inds it] down to the glowing illusion' in an imaginative attempt to give Urizen visionary 'Form', Urizen continues to preside in ungraspable and unshakable transcendence over the poem's confined natural world (*CPP* 94; *CP* 272).

Los's creative labours in *The Book of Los* are thus miserably ambivalent: in one sense, Los's work fashions Urizen's abstract and formless transcendences into artistic form, as he builds a body for him in 'CHAP: IV' (*CPP* 93–4; *CP* 271–2), but in another sense it reduplicates and reproduces Urizen's divisive and oppressive creations. The fact that 'Truth has bounds. Error none' (*CPP* 92; *CP* 269), as the poem says of Los's 'fall' from Urizenic fixity in 'CHAP: II', means that Los is paradoxically enjoined *at once* to resist Urizen's 'bounds' *and* to institute *artistic* 'bounds' around his abstract formlessness, giving a 'Human' shape to his chaos. This 'Human' shape, nevertheless, remains an 'Illusion' (*CPP* 94; *CP* 272), and rehearses Urizenic delusion rather than securing visionary freedom from it. The poet-prophet, then, becomes an ideologue, a priestly proponent of religious limitation who confines infinity within bounds. The fact that the poet-prophet *can* become a priestly ideologue lies, of course, behind Blake's revisionary reading and reinvention of John Milton in *Milton: A Poem in [1]2 Books* (*c.* 1804–1810/11), as we will see in the next chapter; for, in that poem, Blake strives to rescue and reclaim Milton's *rebel* energy from its petrification in reactionary religious ideology.

In *The Book of Los* – as in *The [First] Book of Urizen* and *The Book of Ahania* – Blake rewrites and reclaims the biblical text in a gesture of desacralization that debunks its authority, and reimagines the sacred book for contemporary history and contemporary artistic practice. The *political* gesture of the Lambeth 'Books' is, then, a reconversion of what *The Marriage* calls 'sacred codes' (*CPP* 34; *CP* 181) into 'poetic tales' (*CPP* 38; *CP* 186). However, the struggle of the poet-prophet against the repetition of ideological illusion belongs ongoingly to what we call history and what Blake calls 'eternity'.

5

Contemporary Epics: *'Vala'*, or *'The Four Zoas'*, *Milton: A Poem*

In 1798, Blake writes:

> To defend the Bible in this year 1798 would cost a man his life
> The Beast & the Whore rule without controls . . .
> I have been commanded from Hell not to print this as it is what our Enemies wish (*CPP* 611)

Blake delivers this comment at the start of his fierce annotations to Bishop Richard Watson's *Apology for the Bible* (1797): a text in which Watson, the Bishop of Llandaff, attacked Tom Paine for his sceptical critique of the Bible in *The Age of Reason* of 1794–5. Yet to Blake the bishop's 'Apology' is the ploy of a 'Priest' or 'State trickster' (*CPP* 612) who uses the Bible as an instrument of 'State Religion' (*CPP* 613) and social control – and not, as we have seen Blake doing in the Lambeth 'Books', as a text of radical inspiration and contemporary political reimagining. That the Bible *was* – as he once described it to Samuel Palmer – the 'book of liberty'[1] for Blake meant that any 'defence' of it in the late 1790s was indeed a fearful exercise: for these years saw radical political critique and dissent in Britain fall under brutal State suppression and surveillance against the background of Government fears of the spread of revolutionary activity from France, and the background of the counter-revolutionary and imperial war that raged between France and Britain from 1793 onwards. That Blake is 'commanded from Hell not to print' his attack on the bishop is a measure both of the general political anxiety of the time, and of Blake's sense of his own danger as a 'republican' artist beneath a repressively 'Urizenic' political regime.

Blake, in fact, did not 'print' another illuminated book between *The Song of Los*, *The Book of Los* and *The Book of Ahania* in 1795, and the title pages of *Milton* and *Jerusalem* in the mid 1800s. This silence had to do not merely with Blake's lack of commercial success as a printer of his own books, or the depression of the book market because of the war with France, but with a climate in which the Government suspended habeas corpus in 1794, passed laws against 'treasonable and seditious Practices' and 'Seditious Meetings and Assemblies' in 1795 (Pitt's notorious 'Two Acts'), put radicals like Blake on trial for treason, flooded the capital with spies and informers, and required that every printing press in the country be licensed.[2] Blake's commandment from Hell not to 'print' his evisceration of Bishop Watson came, moreover, in the very year – 1798 – that his friend and erstwhile publisher, Joseph Johnson, was sentenced to nine months' imprisonment for publishing and selling an anti-war pamphlet by the Rev. Gilbert Wakefield. Blake's 'Nervous Fear' (*CPP* 708), as he described it in a letter of 1800 to John Flaxman, was well founded.

But though Blake was not printing poetry in these years, he was writing it. Between 1795 and 1797, he worked on one of the largest engraving commissions he ever received: painting watercolours, and engraving designs, for a sumptuous edition of Edward Young's popular meditative poem *Night Thoughts* (1742–5). The scale of the engraving project was aborted, but the form of Young's poem – structured as a series of nine 'Nights' – inspired Blake to title his new epic poem in deliberate imitation: 'VALA or The Death and Judgement of the [Eternal] Ancient Man a DREAM of Nine Nights' (*CP* 273). Blake worked on this epic from the mid 1790s to the mid 1800s, but the poem was never etched or published (though some of its lines were reworked for inclusion in *Milton* and *Jerusalem*) – and it survives as an extraordinary manuscript palimpsest of revisions, additions, insertions, erasures and reworkings, peppered by equally extraordinary pencil drawings (some of them partially erased by a later owner) of an often graphic sexual nature.[3] Alongside the huge number of textual revisions in the manuscript, Blake revised the title of the poem itself during his work on it, renaming the whole: 'THE FOUR ZOAS The torments of Love & Jealousy in The Death and Judgement of Albion the Ancient Man' (*CPP* 300; *CP* 273). Importantly, the personified figure of 'Albion' is introduced here – for 'Albion' is Blake's name in his epic works for both the visionary form of universal humanity *and* the collective form of England's social body ('Albion' being an archaic or poetic name for Britain). The torment and tragedy of Albion in the poem is that he suffers from what he calls 'war within my members' (*CPP* 388; *CP* 440) – as his constituent and mutual parts (who are the people of England *together* with the populations and nations of Blake's contemporary Europe) fall into general and catastrophic conflict. That in Blake's mythic frame this traumatic conflict rages within the *universal* body of humanity – the body of the 'Ancient Man' – means that the poem is able to move fluidly between historical, social and psychical levels of meaning simultaneously in a grand sweep of visionary personification. Written during the first phase of Britain's and France's revolutionary – and then Napoleonic – wars, '*Vala*', or '*The Four Zoas*' is fixated by the condition of 'war' precisely because *this is the reality of Blake's contemporary Europe*. The narrative framework of the poem, though, is an attempt to envisage a passage *through* the terrible nightmare of the 'war of swords' and *towards* what Blake calls 'intellectual War' (*CPP* 407; *CP* 476); that is, towards the vigorous debates and disputes of cultural activity and artistic vision in a future of fraternal peace.

Briefly, in 1802, the Peace of Amiens brought a cessation of the war between Britain and France before the conflict resumed in 1803 – and, in the preliminaries of that peace in late 1801, Blake wrote to his friend, the artist John Flaxman: 'The Reign of Literature & the Arts Commences . . . I hope that France & England will henceforth be as One Country and their Arts One, & that you will Ere long be erecting Monuments in Paris – Emblems of Peace' (*CPP* 717–18). Blake's wish for Britain and France to be as 'One Country' and their 'Arts One' informs the complex longing in '*Vala*', or '*The Four Zoas*' for Los and Albion to surmount their 'fall into Division', or internal war, and attain 'Resurrection to Unity' (*CPP* 301; *CP* 274) – as, at the poem's close, 'sweet Science reigns' (*CPP* 407; *CP* 476) and the 'Bloody Deluge' gives way to 'living flames winged with intellect' (*CPP*

388; *CP* 440). Albion, as both England and the 'Universal Man' (*CPP* 301; *CP* 274), is rifted by divisions and disasters caused by the internal political war in Britain *and* by the military conflict between European peoples who *should*, for Blake, be united. In a real sense, Albion in the poem is a *victim* of the aggressively contending parties inside him: he is a divided and suffering figure who yearns for 'Unity', but is subjected to the violent contentions and 'Universal Confusion' (*CPP* 388; *CP* 440) of contemporary imperial war. Potentially unitary yet historically divided, Albion bemoans his condition in a keen that echoes the lament for unity uttered by figures such as Ahania in *The Book of Ahania* and Eno in *The Book of Los* (see chapter 4). Thus Albion wails to Urizen – who, in '*Vala*', or '*The Four Zoas*', is a composite allegory of British King and State Religion –

> Arise O stony form of Death O dragon of the Deeps
> Lie down before my feet O Dragon let Urizen arise
> O how couldst thou deform those beautiful proportions
> Of life & person . . .
> My anger against thee is greater than against this Luvah
> For war is [honest] energy Enslavd but thy religion
> The first author of this war & the distracting of honest minds
> Into confused perturbation & strife & honour & pride
> Is a deceit so detestable that I will cast thee out
> If thou repentest not . . .

(*CPP* 389–90; *CP* 442–3)

Urizen's 'religion' here is cited by Albion as the cause of the conflict that engulfs him – in an implicit reference both to Britain's war against France and to the violent, warmongering ideology of the 'Church-and-King' brigades that, in the shape of popular mobs, loyalist associations and Government agents, hounded radicals and demonized France in the period. Albion suffers under Urizen's ideology of 'State Religion' to which Blake, in his annotations to Bishop Watson, attributes the 'English Crusade against France' (*CPP* 613) in the 1790s. Albion's reference to 'Luvah', indeed, places the contest between the poem's divided 'Zoas' – or the four 'living creatures' (Greek: *zoon*) who make up the totality of the 'Universal Man' – firmly in the theatre of the contemporary revolutionary wars. For in Blake 'Luvah' is the Zoa, or creature, of passion and energy – his name is a phonetic pun on 'Lover' – and, in *'Vala'*, or *'The Four Zoas'*, he embodies the '[honest] energy Enslavd' of a desiring and aspiring nation: France. In *Jerusalem*, Blake makes this historical link explicit by stating baldly, in a passage on Albion's imperialist aggressions: 'For Luvah is France: the Victim of the Spectres of Albion . . .' (*CPP* 218; *CP* 770). Urizen's State 'religion' and Luvah's revolutionary 'energy', then, contend with each other in *'Vala'*, or *'The Four Zoas'* in a reprise of the symbolic struggles of Urizen and Orc in *America, Europe* and *The Song of Los* (see chapters 3 and 4), and of Urizen and Fuzon in *The Book of Ahania* (see chapter 4); but, in the later epic, these adversaries do battle with ever increasing ferocity and universality.

Blake's historical allegory in *'Vala'*, or *'The Four Zoas'* is more complex and troubled than in the early 1790s prophecies because Luvah-as-France modulates disastrously into what he appears to oppose – just as France, the revolutionary nation, inverts tragically into an aggressively imperialist State in the latter part of the 1790s and early 1800s. As David Erdman argues, Luvah's decline in the poem into an ever more negative 'Orc' (for in *Vala*, Orc is Luvah's 'fallen' form) charts the ways in which 'the Republic of France bec[omes] an aggressive Empire'.[4] Indeed, Erdman says that Orc's story in the poem is an allegorical version of France's catastrophic decline from republicanism into Bonapartism. He writes: 'The militant Orc who, as a rising "son of fire" in 1792, promised to end the empire of lion and wolf is mocked by the militant Orc who, as Napoleon [Bonaparte] in 1799, contends for imperial power, wringing from the poet a cry of dismay: "Why howl the Lion & the Wolf? why do they roam abroad? . . ." [*CPP* 310, *CP* 295]'.[5] In 'Night the Eighth', then – which maps the fall of humankind into total conflict – Orc reptilizes into a destructive 'Serpent' with whom Urizen 'Commun[es] . . . in dark dissimulation' to manufacture the technologies of war: 'Horrible hooks & nets he formd twisting the cords of iron/ And brass & molten metals cast in hollow globes & bor'd/ Tubes in petrific steel & rammd combustibles & wheels/ And chains & pullies fabricated . . .' (*CPP* 373; *CP* 412). These 'Tubes [bor'd] in petrific steel' are just part of the stock – here, naval cannon and land artillery – in a Urizenic and Orcian arsenal of total confrontation. Blake's narrative metaphor for

Luvah-France's serpentine degeneration into Orc is that he has descended into the 'State calld Satan':

> There is a State namd Satan learn distinct to know . . .
> The Difference between States & Individuals of those States
> The State namd Satan can never be redeemd in all Eternity
> But when Luvah in Orc became a Serpent he des[c]ended into
> That State calld Satan . . .
>
> (*CPP* 380; *CP* 425)

In 'Night the Eighth', the 'State calld Satan' (one of unchecked aggression, war and empire) is so fearfully unleashed that 'All futurity/ Seems teeming with Endless destruction never to be repelld', and 'Desperate remorse swallows the present in a quenchless rage' (*CPP* 374; *CP* 412–13). Against the poem's despair at this contemporary historical cataclysm, however – and in a moving moment of Blakean self-allegory – the troubled figure of the artist 'Los' labours patiently to build the 'Walls of Golgonooza', the regenerative city of Art, in a deliverance of history from nightmare:

> The battle howls the terrors fird rage in the work of death
> Enormous Works Los Contemplated inspird by the holy Spirit
> Los builds the Walls of Golgonooza against the stirring battle
>
> (*CPP* 374; *CP* 413)

'Against the stirring battle', Los and his artistic helpmeet, Enitharmon, 'draw [. . .] from out the ranks of war' (*CPP* 371; *CP* 392) the 'piteous victims' (*CPP* 370; *CP* 391) and the 'spectrous dead' – and fashion them anew, giving them 'forms Embodied & Lovely' (*CPP* 371; *CP* 392) in which to live and love. The suffering and raging victims of war are recreated by Los and Enitharmon in 'infant innocence' (*CPP* 371; *CP* 393): they are remade from 'Spectres of the Dead' (*CPP* 369; *CP* 390) into fathers, brothers, infants and friends (*CPP* 371; *CP* 393). Even Urizen is turned from an enemy of Los into a loved infant image:

> Startled was Los he found his Enemy Urizen now
> In his hands. he wonderd that he felt love & not hate
> His whole soul loved him he beheld him an infant
>
> (*CPP* 371; *CP* 393)

In an extraordinary act of imaginative remaking, Urizen is redeemed by the poem's remorseless drive to 'Resurrection to Unity' (*CPP* 301; *CP* 274); and 'Night the Ninth' sees him shaking 'his aged mantles off' and rising 'into the heavens in naked majesty/ In radiant Youth' (*CPP* 391; *CP* 444). Los's and Enitharmon's creative labour transposes the 'work of death' into imaginative 'Works . . . inspird', and turns war into art in a fulfilment of Blake's hopes that, with the peace of 1801, the 'Reign of Literature & the Arts Commences' (*CPP* 717). Blake inscribes his hopes for peace movingly and metafictionally in 'Night the Seventh' of the poem when, describing Los's and Enitharmon's artistic labours towards peace, he images his own work and that of Catherine Blake in the following terms –

> And first [Los] drew a line upon the walls of shining heaven
> And Enitharmon tincturd it with beams of blushing love
>
> (*CPP* 370; *CP* 392)

– for Blake habitually drew the lines, while Catherine coloured the designs, of his engraved works.

Blake's remorselessly resumed work on his fragmentary visionary-historical epic – his revisions, rewritings, additions and insertions – resembles, in fact, nothing so much as Los's *own* flawed and struggling labours towards redemption in the narrative of the poem itself. Indeed, Los broods over the 'Spectres of the Dead' in *'Vala'*, or *'The Four Zoas'* in the same way that Blake labours to find, within the structures of his epic poem, a redemptive form in which to envision and configure a warring, violent, contradictory, chaotic and unpredictable contemporary history. The narrative overlayings of the manuscript, together with its introduction of providential framing devices – that appear for the first time in Blake's work here, such as 'Beulah', the 'Council of God' and the 'Seven Eyes of God' – all bespeak an artistic struggle on Blake's part to fashion an unmanageable history into aesthetic form.

Blake began *'Vala'*, or *'The Four Zoas'* in the mid 1790s at Lambeth, before leaving for Felpham – but his work on the poem, or an incarnation of it, continued during the Felpham years. In 1803, for instance, he writes to Thomas Butts of an epic poem he has been composing that introduces a new symbolic 'Machinery' into the literary world: 'I have in these three years composed an immense number of verses on One Grand Theme Similar to Homers Illiad or Miltons Paradise Lost the Persons & Machinery intirely new to the Inhabitants of Earth . . . My heart is full of futurity' (*CPP* 728–9). This work is almost certainly *'Vala'*, or *'The Four Zoas'*, but it is likely that the 'One Grand Theme' of the verses includes the germ of *Milton: A Poem in [1]2 Books* (*c.* 1804–1810/11), too, for Blake dated the title page of *Milton* '1804' – just one year after his departure from Felpham.

Blake left for Felpham in September 1800 to take up patronage and employment under the poet and biographer William Hayley, and, as we saw in chapter 3, he speaks to John Flaxman in the month of his departure from London of the 'Nervous Fear' (*CPP* 708) that has afflicted him in that city. A recently discovered and newly published letter by Blake to his friend George Cumberland in the same month (just three weeks before the move to Felpham) reinforces this sense of the political fear and darkness with which Blake associated London at the end of the 1790s. In the prose part of the letter, Blake speaks of 'Londons accursed walls', while in the verse section (quoted here in full) he writes:

> Dear Generous Cumberland nobly solicitous for a Friends welfare. Behold me
> Whom your Friendship has Magnified: Rending the manacles of Londons Dungeon dark
> I have rent the black net & escap'd. See My Cottage at Felpham in joy
> Beams over the Sea, a bright light over France, but the Web & the Veil I have left
> Behind me at London resists every beam of light; hanging from heaven to Earth
> Dropping with human gore. Lo! I have left it! I have torn it from my Limbs
> I shake my wings ready to take my flight! Pale, Ghastly pale: stands the City in fear[6]

As we saw in his annotations to Watson, Blake mourned the raging rule of the 'Beast & the Whore' in Pitt's London at the end of the 1790s – but, as Jon Mee says, 'Disillusionment with France after 1795 as a potential liberator for "the captive in chains & the poor in the prison" [*CPP* 325; *CP* 320] [that] is a familiar part of the story of the Romantic reaction to the Revolution' is *not* a part of Blake's story here. Mee indicates, indeed, that Blake's letter suggests that he 'harboured [political] hopes from that quarter [France] as late as 1800'.[7] In a double effect of syntax in his poem, Blake suggests both that his 'Cottage at Felpham . . . Beams over the Sea' in visionary joy, and that there 'Beams over the Sea, a bright light over France' – hinting that political illumination may yet come from the revolutionary nation, in contrast to the benighted, imprisoning and fearful capital of Britain. The hope and liberty brought by Blake's move to Felpham in 1800 (though Felpham would, of course, become yet another prison that would drive him back to London in 1803) is measured in part by the new poem he conceived and symbolically played out in the Felpham years – *Milton: A Poem in [1]2 Books.* Though *Milton* is, in Blake's words to Hayley in 1805, a visionary 'history of my Spiritual Sufferings' (*CPP* 767) at Felpham, it is also a poem in which he recovers and reclaims a radical vision and sense of revolutionary purpose through critically identifying with his great republican forebear, John Milton (1608–74).

In *Milton,* John 'Milton' is, for Blake, the pre-eminent artist and prophet of spiritual vision and political liberation in English poetry. The most celebrated comment in the Romantic period on Milton as a revolutionary figure comes, indeed, from Blake himself – for in *The Marriage of Heaven and Hell* Blake writes: 'Note. The reason Milton wrote in fetters when he wrote of Angels & God, and at liberty when of Devils & Hell, is because he was a true Poet and of the Devils party without knowing it' (*CPP* 35; *CP* 182). Here, Blake offers a vision of Milton as a deeply divided figure: on the one hand, he is a conservative, reactionary English Puritan 'fettered' to theological dogma – subscribing to an 'Angelic' code of religious law and punishment – but on the other hand he is a subversive figure whose poetry embodies the diabolical, republican energies of the anti-monarchical English Revolution of which he is a part as both polemicist and apologist. And Blake, embracing the rebel Milton, finds *Milton the revolutionary* symbolically encoded in the figure of 'Satan' in his *Paradise Lost* (1674); for, although Satan is the opponent of Miltonic Heaven in the poem, he is also presented by Milton as a sublime figure of indomitable energy and unquenchable political aspiration. Depicted in heroic terms, Satan the rebel angel in *Paradise Lost* is for Blake an image of Milton himself as a rebel artist and political revolutionary, defying authority and tradition and celebrating the creative energy of insurrectionary desire. As Blake's first biographer, Alexander Gilchrist, records a friend of Blake's saying: 'He loved liberty . . . His sympathies were with Milton . . . not with Milton as to his puritanism, but his love of a grand ideal scheme of republicanism'.[8] Milton is a 'true Poet' for Blake, then, on the levels both of art and politics – he is of the 'Devils party', as a figure of creative rebel energy and republican revolt, even though his Puritan self does not 'know' it.

This *divided* Milton of *The Marriage* is very much the conflicted protagonist of Blake's *Milton* – and the strategy of the latter poem is to intervene correctively in the history of Milton's career and reputation, and to reinvent him *away from orthodoxy* in a radical or rebel direction, in a new prophetic and regenerative mode for Blake's own historical period (just as Blake reconfigures the Bible in the Lambeth 'Books' for his contemporary history). As with Blake's reinvention of the discourse of spiritual and political apocalypse of the seventeenth-century Civil War revolutionaries in his historical prophecies of the early 1790s, his reclamation of Milton in *Milton* is part of a resurgent language of apocalyptic republicanism – all the more urgent, in Blake's terms, in the context of the dark night of European politics of the 1800s, as we have seen it unfolded in the rifted mythic-historical epic *'Vala'*, or *'The Four Zoas'*. In his sonnet 'London, 1802', William Wordsworth mourns the loss of republican political inspiration in the dispirited England of 1802, and declaims, 'Milton! thou should'st be living at this hour:/ England hath need of thee . . .' (ll. 1–2); but the gesture of Blake's *Milton*, against Wordsworth's lament, is to assert that Milton *is* still 'living' (or his radical inspiration is), for Blake's poem envisions a revivification of this inspiration in the political present.

John Milton needs, however – Blake's *Milton* asserts – to be reborn both historically and spiritually. At the start of Blake's epic, we learn that Milton has 'walkd about in Eternity/ One hundred years' after his historical death, 'pondring the intricate mazes of Providence'. Crucially, though, the story of Milton's immortal life is that he is 'Unhappy tho in heav'n' (*CPP* 96; *CP* 515). Like his own rebel hero Satan in *Paradise Lost*, 'Milton' in *Milton* is discontented under the regimen of heaven; and the iconoclastic gesture of Blake's poem is to reimagine in a new, radical theodicy (where Milton himself 'falls' voluntarily from the orthodox empyrean back to earth to redeem his Puritan errors) the expulsion of the rebel host from Milton's heaven. Milton in *Milton*, therefore, leaps meteorically and exultantly from 'the Zenith as a falling star' (*CPP* 110; *CP* 543) in an ironic echo and reappropriation of the rebel angel Mulciber's fall in *Paradise Lost*: 'with the setting Sun [he]/ Dropt from the Zenith like a falling Star' (Bk 1, ll. 744–5). In *Milton*, then, Milton actively *spurns* orthodox heaven – rather than is expelled from it – and embraces in a rebel fall an adventure in self-reinvention.

But what is it that prompts Milton's 'unexampled deed' of self-remaking in *Milton*? The answer Blake gives is: 'A Bards prophetic Song!' In *Milton*'s narrative, Milton hears the 'Song' of a nameless Bard sung 'at eternal tables' (*CPP* 96; *CP* 515), and this Song induces in him a moment of mournful self-revelation in which the nature of his own orthodox errors (in Blakean terms) is disclosed to him; and, as a result, he '[rises] up from the heavens of Albion ardorous', '[takes] off the robe of the promise, . . . ungird[s] himself from the oath of God' (*CPP* 108; *CP* 539), and plunges from heaven in a transforming divestment of his orthodox, Puritan, patriarchal self. The Bard's Song runs from Plate 2 to Plate 14 (*CPP* 96–108; *CP* 515–39) of 'Book the First' of *Milton*, and is a complex, oblique allegory of poetic dispute in heaven in which three Sons of Los – Satan, Rintrah, Palamabron – are embroiled in an argument about their respective roles and places in the imaginative labours of eternity. Essentially, this dispute is provoked by Satan – who usurps Palamabron's 'station' (*CPP* 100; *CP* 523), and seeks supremacy over his brothers. Like Urizen in *The [First] Book of Urizen*, Satan disrupts the republican, egalitarian order of eternity, and aggressively asserts his own pre-eminence by declaring: 'I am God alone/ There is no other!' (*CPP* 103; *CP* 529). The fact that Satan *does* this in the Bard's Song indicates that Blake submits the figure of Satan in *Milton* to profound rethinking; for Satan has turned from the fiery, creative 'Devil' of *The Marriage of Heaven and Hell* into a tyrant of vaunting self-righteousness. In effect, Satan has traced the path from radical to reactionary mapped by Blake in the stories of Fuzon-turned-god in *The Book of Ahania* (chapter 4), and Orc-turned-serpent in *'Vala'*, or *'The Four Zoas'*. Ideologically, Satan has moved from insurrectionist to supremacist, from rebel to tyrant; and the historical – and revolutionary – process in which radicalism inverts disastrously into repression, as in the stories of Robespierre or Napoleon, is never far from Blake's eye here. The fact that 'Satan' means 'adversary' in Hebrew alerts us to the fact that, in the 1800s, the 'adversary' for Blake *is* orthodoxy and an endemic political repression.

Blake returns, then, to John Milton – and to the spiritual and political revolution of an earlier period – in order to re-envision liberty in a dark night of ideological retrenchment in the 1800s. But despite Milton's prophetic status, Blake finds the 'Satan' of his contemporary world *already* inhabiting Milton the seventeenth-century revolutionary, and that is why Milton must be made anew by Blake for his own time: it is why he must cast off the 'Satanic' errors that inhabit him so he can become a vehicle for revolutionary vision in William Blake's historical moment. And it is the Bard's Song of *Milton* that shows Milton the nature of his own errors, the false body that he must divest himself of to embrace regeneration. After the Bard's Song ends, 'Milton' declares in revelatory self-recognition: 'I in my Selfhood am that Satan: I am that Evil One! He is my Spectre!' (*CPP* 108; *CP* 540). The Satanic 'Selfhood' that Milton recognizes in himself is, in fact, the collective body of his Puritanical and patriarchal errors: it is the composite form of his self-righteousness, his masculinism, his vengefulness and, for Blake, his warlike classicism at the level of aesthetic ideology. Milton's 'giving up of Selfhood' (*CPP* 110; *CP* 543) in the poem involves an act of self-remaking that returns him to earth to redeem his errors, and open himself up to revision. The narrative metaphor for this enterprise is that Milton must 'redeem' his 'Sixfold Emanation' called 'Ololon', who is 'scatter'd thro' the deep/ In torment'. Ololon is, among other things, the female aspect of Milton's humanity: and, sundered from her, Milton must reunite with her so he can 'perish' (*CPP* 96; *CP* 515) in his Puritan, masculinist, patriarchal selfhood. Historically, Ololon is the embodiment of Milton's three wives and three daughters, and is 'Sixfold' for that reason. Ololon's separation from Milton in the poem is a composite figure for the historical Milton's vengeful advocacy of divorce, for his repudiation of his Royalist first wife, for his coldness towards the daughters of that marriage – and for what Lucy

Newlyn calls his 'indifference to the feminine'[9] in his poetry. The lost Ololon is also a figure for Milton's separation from the radicalism of his own inspiration – for his relinquishment of his prophetic role through (in Blake's terms) a capitulation to literary classicism and Protestant moralism. As well as revising these errors of the historical Milton, *Milton* also seeks to redeem Milton from what Robert N. Essick and Joseph Viscomi call the 'late eighteenth-century conversion of Milton [from] . . . revolutionary poet-prophet into a versifier of conventional pieties'.[10] One perpetrator of that eighteenth-century reduction of Milton's meaning, for Blake, was his own patron and employer at Felpham, William Hayley, whose *Life of Milton* was published in 1796; and the story of Satan's usurpation of imaginative vision in the Bard's Song of *Milton* is in part an autobiographical allegory of Blake's own sense that the poetaster Hayley, in the role of a repressive 'Satan', has usurped *his* – Blake's – position as the true artist.

In a complex visionary narrative, Milton in *Milton* plummets to earth as a falling star, and enters William Blake (*CPP* 110; *CP* 543) in a stunning identification whereby seventeenth-century precursor and Romantic inheritor are both remade in the present – and in the name of a transformed future. Milton's return to earth takes the form of a quest narrative in which the errant poet-prophet encounters moments of blockage that threaten to halt his 'unexampled deed' of self-transformation. Thus Urizen seeks to impede Milton's progress by 'pouring on/ To [his] brain . . . icy fluid' from the biblical river Jordan – in a grimly negative baptism back into Puritan orthodoxy. Milton's response, though, is to take 'red clay' and 'Creat[e] new flesh on the Demon cold' (*CPP* 112; *CP* 548), imaginatively redeeming rather than aggressively punishing his antagonist. Milton's ultimate test and temptation is by 'Satan' himself – by *'the adversary'* – and when Satan rolls his 'thunders against Milton', Milton confronts him and says:

> Satan! my Spectre! I know my power thee to annihilate
> And be a greater in thy place, & be thy Tabernacle
> A covering for thee to do thy will, till one greater comes
> And smites me as I smote thee & becomes my covering.
> Such are the Laws of thy false Heavns! but Laws of Eternity

> Are not such: know thou: I come to Self Annihilation
> Such are the Laws of Eternity that each shall mutually
> Annihilate himself for others good, as I for thee
>
> (*CPP* 139; *CP* 597–8)

In *Paradise Lost*, Milton hurled Satan into 'bottomless perdition' (Bk 1, l. 47), and consigned him to Hell in a gesture of, in Blakean terms, destructive, vengeful and tyrannical self-righteousness. In Blake's hands now, though, Milton *refuses to punish Satan*, and forgives him instead; and this, in Blake's antinomian logic of ethico-historical apocalypse, enables an alternative history to be opened up, and a new possible historical futurity to dawn. Instead of Milton's *repeating* Satan – and taking his 'place' in simultaneous suppression and repetition of him – Blake's Milton 'Annihilates' his 'Self' so that the story of revolution's reversal into repression, or of rebellion's inversion into tyranny, can be decisively rewritten in the name of an alternative future. When Milton forgives Satan here – and annihilates his 'Self righteousness' (*CPP* 139; *CP* 599) before him – we witness not just the regeneration of the Puritan Milton wedded to a disastrous theology of punishment, but of the political Milton who, in 1649, justified the regicide of Charles I as a 'well-pleasing Sacrifice'[11] to God, and who acted as a servant of the warmongering Cromwellian Protectorate. In Blake's *Milton*, John Milton discards his Puritan self-righteousness and his political vengefulness, and is recreated by Blake into a new, prophetic, radical force in history. Thus the providential 'Seven Angels of the Presence' (*CPP* 131; *CP* 584) in the poem declare Milton to be 'a State about to be Created/ Called Eternal Annihilation' (*CPP* 132; *CP* 585), for Milton the revolutionary returns to earth in Blake's epic to *reinvent revolution* itself – not as a story of war and revenge but, in the words of Milton's lost inspiration and Emanation Ololon, as a 'striving/ In Self annihilation [to] giv[e] thy life to thy enemies' (*CPP* 141; *CP* 602).

And *Milton* ends with an extraordinary antinomian apocalypse that fuses John Milton's spiritual regeneration with a new, rewritten Christian nativity – a new revelatory historical incarnation of 'Jesus the Saviour' (*CPP* 143; *CP* 606). That incarnation results from Milton's climactic *reunion* with his lost Emanation and inspiration, Ololon. In the closing stages of *Milton*'s narrative, the poem's visionary drama unfolds literally in Blake's 'Garden/ Before [his] Cottage' (*CPP* 137; *CP* 594) at Felpham – where Ololon appears in vision to Blake as a 'Virgin of twelve years' (*CPP* 137; *CP* 593), and Blake says to her, 'Virgin of Providence fear not to enter into my Cottage' (*CPP* 137; *CP* 594). Blake's words echo the angel Gabriel's injunction to the virgin Mary in the nativity story to 'Fear not' (Luke 1:30) at the divine birth that is to be conceived in her; for Ololon herself is to conceive 'Jesus the Saviour' (*CPP* 143; *CP* 606) in a new birth through her reunion with Milton, her father, lover, husband and friend. And Milton, like Ololon, appears in Blake's garden, too – 'descending down into my Cottage/ Garden: clothed in black, severe & silent he descended' (*CPP* 138; *CP* 597). Here, Milton is dressed in black Puritan garb in the manner that he was depicted in most contemporary portraits; but, as with Ololon's appearance in 'Virgin' form, this is a clothing or embodiment that he is about to 'cast off' to reveal what Blake calls the naked 'Human Lineaments' (*CPP* 142; *CP* 603–5).[12] Consequently, in a climax that is at once spiritual and sexual, the historical Milton's overvaluation of bodily chastity is blown apart as the Puritan Milton joins with the Virgin Ololon in an apocalyptic sexual consummation *and* millennial birth. Virgin hymen and Puritan 'Shadow' are both divided and dispersed in an overwhelming mutual encounter:

> . . . the Virgin divided Six-fold & with a shriek . . .
> Away from Ololon she divided & fled into the depths
> Of Miltons Shadow as a Dove upon the stormy Sea.
>
> Then as a Moony Ark Ololon descended to Felphams Vale
> In clouds of blood, in streams of gore, with dreadful thunderings
> Into the Fires of Intellect that rejoic'd in Felphams Vale
> Around the Starry Eight: with one accord the Starry Eight became
> One Man Jesus the Saviour. wonderful! round his limbs
> The Clouds of Ololon folded as a Garment dipped in blood
> Written within & without in woven letters: & the Writing
> Is the Divine Revelation in the Litteral expression:
> A Garment of War, I heard it namd the Woof of Six Thousand Years
>
> (*CPP* 143; *CP* 605–6)

In this remarkable vision, Milton's and Ololon's coming together gives birth to the 'eschatological meaning'[13] of history itself, and to the revelation of 'Jesus the Saviour' – who appears here in a bloody nativity scene, folded about by the crimson clouds of Ololon's parturient flesh. The 'Garment dipped in blood' out of which Jesus emerges and in which he is clothed is an apocalyptic text-ure 'written within & without', for it is made of a sublime, revelatory textuality without concealment – a revelation of history 'in the Litteral expression', and a vision of historical time in its totality ('the Woof of Six Thousand Years', in Blake's shorthand for history).[14] This sublime revelation causes 'Terror' to 'str[ike] in the Vale', for Blake falls 'outstretchd upon the path/ A moment', his soul returning then 'To Resurrection & Judgment in the Vegetable Body'. Collapsed by the enormity and extremity of this vision, Blake blanks out on the path of his cottage garden in Felpham some time between 1800 and 1803, viewing in vision Milton's and Ololon's regenerative 'acts by me unknown' (*CPP* 141; *CP* 602) – and then his wife, Catherine Blake, appears by his side, disturbed ('my sweet Shadow of Delight stood trembling by my side': *CPP* 143; *CP* 606). Blake comes back to consciousness after 'A moment', though, in an abrupt return of apocalypse to history, for the textual 'Garment of War' that *is* history here is still to be woven, still to be revealed, and still to be written as the historical 'Woof' of six thousand years.

William Blake's *Milton: A Poem*, then, together with John Milton's *Paradise Lost*, becomes part of the weave of this huge historical texture – this immense labour of apocalyptic-historical inscription. And the vision with which *Milton* ends – and which 'Milton' himself engenders in his unexampled return to history – is an apocalyptic inscription in a revelation to come.

6

Social Epic: *Jerusalem: The Emanation of the Giant Albion*

In his 'Preface' to *Milton: A Poem*, Blake urges the artists of the 'New Age' to combat 'Corporeal' and promote 'Mental . . . War' (*CPP* 95; *CP* 513), and follows this impassioned cultural manifesto with the lyric, 'And did those feet in ancient time'.[1] The lyric ends:

> I will not cease from Mental Fight,
> Nor shall my Sword sleep in my hand:
> Till we have built Jerusalem,
> In Englands green & pleasant Land.
>
> (*CPP* 96; *CP* 514)

Blake's building of 'Jerusalem' – in Hebrew, the 'abode of peace' – through 'Mental Fight' is the unceasing labour of his radical art from the early *Songs* to the late epics, as we have seen. And, after 1803, when he returned to London from Felpham, it was the imaginative work of the frequently dark years leading up to 1820, too, ending in the production of his final and major illuminated poem – itself called *Jerusalem* (*c.* 1804–20). Blake dated the title page of *Jerusalem: The Emanation of the Giant Albion* 1804, like *Milton*; but after initial rapid progress on the poem up to 1807, the work was produced haltingly over many years, and no complete copies of it were printed until the end of the 1810s.

Although he printed five copies of *Jerusalem*, Blake only ever fully coloured one, and this remained unsold at his death in 1827. By 1807, though, it seems Blake had etched a substantial number of the final 100 plates of the poem, for in a notebook entry of that year his friend George Cumberland wrote: 'Blake has eng.[d] 60 Plates of a new Prophecy!'[2] In 1809, in his *Descriptive Catalogue* for his ill-fated exhibition of that year, Blake refers to a work '[t]he Artist has written ... and will, if God please, publish' that tells the story of a symbolic 'fourfold' man who was 'originally one', but became 'self-divided': his story is one of 'great sublimity and pathos', and contains 'the ancient history of Britain, and the world of Satan and of Adam' (*CPP* 543). This work is undoubtedly *Jerusalem*, for Blake's description isolates two defining features of the poem: the 'self-division' of 'Albion' or Britain, and the mapping of British history on to biblical topology and typology.

In 1811, Blake showed parts of what Robert Southey described as 'a perfectly mad poem called Jerusalem' to the future poet laureate – and Southey commented scornfully on what he saw: 'Oxford Street is in Jerusalem'.[3] The detail to which Southey refers – in 'Chap: 2' of *Jerusalem* – is a description of the visionary 'Gate of Los', which bends 'across the road of Oxford Street' (*CPP* 181; *CP* 701). For all its contemptuousness, though, Southey's remark identifies an important aspect of the rhetorical mode of *Jerusalem*; namely, its mapping of a literal on to a symbolic geography. Throughout *Jerusalem*, 'Albion' is presented in a state of miserably aggressive division – separated, as Milton is in *Milton*, from his 'Emanation', who is called 'Jerusalem'. The sundering of Albion and Jerusalem in *Jerusalem* is figured schematically in a minute and elaborate set of geographical and symbolic correspondences between British and biblical place names and personae (see Plates 71–2: *CPP* 224–7; *CP* 784–90) – and the very distances between the terms of these correspondences is a measure, in the poem's logic, of the need for spiritual reintegration. In *'Vala'*, or *'The Four Zoas'*, Jerusalem is described as 'a City yet a Woman' (*CPP* 391; *CP* 46), and she is that in *Jerusalem*, too, at once a place and personification, and this means that Albion's division from her can be figured *simultaneously* in geographical and in psychical terms. As a symbolic value, indeed, Jerusalem is 'in' London (to adopt Southey's terms) as a visionary or regenerative potentiality: in general, she is a utopian figure for political, mental, spiritual and sexual liberty. Thus Blake declares in a motto inscribed at the end of 'Chap: 1': 'SUCH VISIONS HAVE APPEARD TO ME/ AS I MY ORDERD RACE HAVE RUN/ JERUSALEM IS NAMED LIBERTY/ AMONG THE SONS OF ALBION' (*CPP* 171; *CP* 685).

It is the comprehensive *loss* of 'liberty', though – and of the well-spring of social and political liberty, the 'Human Imagination' (*CPP* 258; *CP* 845) – that Blake charts in *Jerusalem*, and against which he labours in regeneration. In the poem, Blake's poet-prophet 'Los' is a more crucial figure than in any of the other illuminated books; and the account of Los's labour and despair over Albion's collapse into repression, war and oppression movingly allegorizes Blake's troubled relationship, as a radical artist, to the capitalist, militarist and imperialist social body of England that he addresses in the poem. Los's 'Spectre', for instance – namely, his punitive or self-righteous side – counsels Los that he should spurn Albion because Albion 'drinks thee up like water! . . . [and] has divided thee in sunder: and wilt thou still forgive?' (*CPP* 149; *CP* 643–4). Los insists, however – despite the Spectre's 'Pride & Self-righteousness' – that he 'act[s] not for [him]self', but 'for Albions sake' (*CPP* 151; *CP* 647), and he asserts he will remain Albion's friend, working for him in 'anguish of regeneration' and 'terrors of self annihilation' (*CPP* 150; *CP* 646). Los may not reject Albion in the poem, but Albion certainly rejects Los, and this mirrors Blake's own anguished relationship to his contemporary British public.

Thus, at the beginning of *Jerusalem*, a bitter Blakean self-allegory is inscribed materially – or in *literal* form – on the copper plate of the text. Plate 3 of *Jerusalem*, entitled 'To the Public', displays a moment of artistic optimism – no doubt in 1804, following Blake's return from Felpham – in which Blake expresses confidence in his expected audience. He writes:

> After my three years slumber on the banks of the Ocean, I again display my Giant forms to the Public: My former Giants & Fairies having receiv'd the highest reward possible: the [*love*] and [*friendship*] of those with whom to be connected, is to be [*blessed*]: I cannot doubt that this more consolidated & extended Work, will be as kindly received . . .
>
> . . . Therefore [*Dear*] Reader, [*forgive*] what you do not approve, & [*love*] me for this energetic exertion of my talent. (*CPP* 145; *CP* 636)

The italicized words in this passage are acidic, *material erasures* on the copper plate (see *IB* 282; *CIB* 300); for, at some point, Blake literally scored out a string of words – 'love', 'friendship', 'blessed', 'Dear', 'forgive', 'love' – that were expressive of the artist's faith in the 'Public' he addresses. The gaps on the plate are, in this way, caustic material marks of the poet's disillusionment and estrangement from the social body – the England or 'Albion' – to which he speaks: they are the literal inscription of Blake's alienation from the 'Public' whose love, friendship and imagination he courts and desires, but by whom he is spurned. If Los's Spectre, as we saw, insists to him that Albion 'has divided [him] in sunder' and deserves punishment, then the mutilation of *Jerusalem* Plate 3 is a mark *in the historical real* of the sundering of William Blake's love, talent and enthusiasm from his audience; it betokens his social division from 'Albion'. Like 'Jerusalem' herself *in Jerusalem,* Blake is exiled from the political body to which he speaks. As Morton D. Paley comments: 'The gaps on the plate were like wounds that could never heal. When Blake sold a monochrome copy of *Jerusalem* to his friend John Linnell, he could have supplied the missing words in black ink, but he did not choose to do so. Plate 3 would remain, in Jerome McGann's words, a "broken text", emblematic in this respect of *Jerusalem* as a whole'.[4]

Robert N. Essick suggests that it was 'probably during [the] dark years'[5] of the early 1810s that Blake gouged out the words on Plate 3; for, in Alexander Gilchrist's phrase, these were 'Years of Deepening Neglect'[6] that followed a string of disappointments in Blake's public ambitions. These included his disastrous one-man exhibition of sixteen paintings at Broad Street, Golden Square, in 1809 – for which he wrote *A Descriptive Catalogue of Blake's Exhibition* (*CPP* 526–51). Blake secured no sales from this exhibition and solicited just one review by way of public notice, and this was a poisonous attack by Robert Hunt in *The Examiner* that was as personally abusive (Blake is 'an unfortunate lunatic, whose personal inoffensiveness secures him from confinement'[7]) as it was critically dismissive. In Blake's *Jerusalem,* then, Robert Hunt (along with his two brothers, Leigh and John, joint editors of *The Examiner*) earns a place among the accusing and punishing 'Sons of Albion' (twelve in number, these 'Sons' are desperately negative versions of the biblical twelve tribes of Israel) under the name of 'Hand': for the Hunt brothers' editorial signature in *The Examiner* was a hand with a pointing finger. In a characteristic visionary response, Blake reads the 'Hand' symbol of the Hunt brothers as a sign of accusation; and, indeed,

the Sons of Albion in *Jerusalem* are a vengeful collective of punishers and aggressors who lacerate Albion and resist Los. Thus Los says: 'Hand sits before his furnace: scorn of others & furious pride/ ... indignant self-righteousness .../ Rose up against me thundering ...' (*CPP* 150; *CP* 646).

Along with Hand, the Sons of Albion include 'Hyle & Coban ... Kwantok, Peachey, Brereton, Slayd & Hutton ... Scofield! Kox, Kotope and Bowen' (*CPP* 147; *CP* 640); and at least six of these accusers owe their names to an event, the most traumatic of Blake's life, that symbolized for him the violence and derangement of 'Albion' – Blake's indictment and trial in 1803–4 on charges of sedition, from an accusation brought against him by a disgraced soldier, Private John Scholfield, who alleged, in August 1803, that Blake damned the king and soldiery of England when ejecting him from his garden at Felpham.[8] Blake was acquitted of this charge at Chichester in January 1804, but the episode encapsulated to him the cruelty and paranoia of an 'Albion' in the grip of panic fear about invasion from France during the summer of 1803 – following the resumption of war between France and Britain in May of that year.

Blake read his trial for sedition, indeed, as a symptom of Albion's punishment of his own members – and of England's severance from the imaginative vision or political realization of peace and liberty (figured in the poem in Albion's exiled 'Emanation', Jerusalem). Composed and etched over many years, most of which saw Britain embroiled in the 'War of Blood' (*CPP* 199; *CP* 736) with Napoleonic France, *Jerusalem* – like *Europe: A Prophecy* and *The [First] Book of Urizen* in the mid 1790s – anatomizes the *ideological* underpinnings (for Blake, the *spiritual* causes) of war, empire and social repression in Britain and Europe. Thus each of *Jerusalem*'s four chapters is prefaced by an address 'to' the constituent members of Albion's ideological and social body. After 'To the Public' that precedes 'Chap: 1', we encounter 'To the Jews' prefacing 'Chap: 2' (*CPP* 171–4; *CP* 685–9), 'To the Deists' prefacing 'Chap 3' (*CPP* 200–202; *CP* 737–9), and 'To the Christians' prefacing 'C 4' (*CPP* 231–3; *CP* 797–9). 'To the Jews' is an impassioned argument against the exclusionary nature of Jewish religion, and draws on the cabbalistic tradition of 'Adam Kadmon' – the primordial man who, Blake says, 'containd in his mighty limbs all things in

Heaven & Earth' – to affirm the 'One Religion' of humankind (for Blake the self-annihilating 'Religion of Jesus': *CPP* 171; *CP* 685) in an echo of the universalizing arguments of *All Religions are One* (see chapter 2). Against this, Albion's exclusionary self-righteousness in *Jerusalem* embodies the law-bound religion of the Old Testament in the form of social and political violence – as Albion turns away from the 'Universal Family' (*CPP* 180; *CP* 699) in vengeful self-assertion. 'To the Deists' attacks, among other things, the links between deism and political statecraft – for Blake considers deism to be a religion of spiritual and political self-justification that supports war and oppression through alignment with State ideology. The 'Deists', Blake asserts, 'acquit & flatter the Alexanders & Caesars, the Lewis's & Fredericks' who promote social and imperial 'War' as the self-serving logic of the State: 'All the Destruction . . . in Christian Europe has arisen from Deism', he asserts (*CPP* 201; *CP* 738–9). Religion as State ideology *is* 'Deism' for Blake – as his inclusion of Louis XVI of France ('Lewis') and Frederick the Great of Prussia ('Frederick') among its ideologues shows. 'To the Christians', on the other hand, is a passionate Blakean redefinition of Christianity as the exercise of the 'Divine Arts of Imagination' (*CPP* 231; *CP* 797) – and as the engagement in 'Mental pursuit for the Building up of Jerusalem' (*CPP* 232; *CP* 798). This, in contrast to a warlike and statist 'Deism', involves what 'To the Jews' calls the return from 'cruel Sacrifices' to 'Mental Sacrifice & War' (*CPP* 174; *CP* 688–9).

In *Jerusalem*, Albion's enchainment to a warmongering, sacrificial creed mires him in the psychology and politics of punishment, and this results in his spiritual death. Albion, then, is dead or sleeping for much of the poem's narrative, and Blake's insistent call throughout the epic is for 'England' to 'awake! awake! awake!/ Jerusalem thy Sister calls!/ Why wilt thou sleep the sleep of death?' (*CPP* 233; *CP* 799). In a moment of terrified and revelatory recognition at the end of 'Chap: 2', Blake declares:

> Hark! the mingling cries of Luvah with the Sons of Albion
> Hark! & Record the terrible wonder! that the Punisher
> Mingles with his Victims Spectre, enslaved and tormented
> To him whom he has murderd, bound in vengeance & enmity

> Shudder not, but Write, & the hand of God will assist you!
> Therefore I write Albions last words. Hope is banish'd from me.
>
> (*CPP* 196; *CP* 729)

Here, the mingling of the murderous shouts of Albion's 'Sons' with the 'cries of Luvah' discloses Blake's reading of the prolonged and bloody history of the Napoleonic Wars (for, as we saw in chapter 5, 'Luvah is France: the Victim of the Spectres of Albion' (*CPP* 218; *CP* 770)) – Wars that raged virtually uninterrupted during the composition of *Jerusalem,* and ended only in 1815, with Napoleon's defeat by British, Prussian and Austrian forces at Waterloo. For Blake, imperial Britain's wars against expansionist Napoleonic France consisted in a 'mingling' of aggressive and punishing 'Spectres': Blake, that is to say, saw the wars as the reciprocal enslavement of contending nations bound to each other in a cycle of violence where the 'Punisher' fuses with the 'Victims Spectre' in mutual 'vengeance & enmity'. About 1808, Blake scrawled in his copy of Reynolds's *Discourses on Art,* 'When France got free Europe 'twixt Fools & Knaves/ Were Savage first to France, & after; Slaves' (*CPP* 641; *CP* 632) – and this encapsulates his account of the way Britain's (and the European monarchies') punishment of revolutionary France in the 1790s inverted into the 'Slavery' of inescapable retributive conflict in the later period. It is striking that Blake presents Albion's 'last words' *as* a direct response to Albion's and Luvah's conflicts: for this suggests that to Blake England's spiritual death is intimately bound up with its attitude towards France.

Jerusalem shows how, in the maelstrom of war, 'Luvah str[ives] to gain dominion over Albion', and how Albion is 'left prostrate' by the 'terrible smitings of Luvah' (*CPP* 192; *CP* 721); but the poem's dominant emphasis is on Los's call to Albion *not* to take vengeance, *not* to pursue retribution, and *not* to inflict punishment on Luvah. Los insists:

> O Albion, if thou takest vengeance; if thou revengest thy wrongs
> Thou art for ever lost! What can I do to hinder the Sons
> Of Albion from taking vengeance? or how shall I them perswade.
>
> (*CPP* 194; *CP* 726)

In *Jerusalem,* Los's demand to Albion to desist from war and retribution is part of a Christian, providential and antinomian call to historical apocalypse in which Albion's and Luvah's regeneration depends on a mutual self-annihilation, and a mutual self-giving. This is the millennial ethics urged upon Albion by the 'Divine Family' (*CPP* 179; *CP* 698) in the poem – for they mercifully pursue Albion as he turns from them in 'Thunders of deadly war', and implore:

> Albion! Our wars are wars of life, & wounds of love,
> With intellectual spears, & long winged arrows of thought:
> Mutual in one anothers love and wrath all renewing
> We live as One Man . . .
> As One Man all the Universal Family; and that One Man
> We call Jesus the Christ: and he in us, and we in him,
> Live in perfect harmony in Eden the land of life,
> Giving, receiving, and forgiving each others trespasses . . .
> If we have offended, forgive us, take not vengeance against us.
> (*CPP* 179–80; *CP* 699)

Here, 'Eden' is the radical republic and egalitarian fraternity of the 'Universal Family' – which includes all and inhabits each in the shape of 'Jesus the Christ', the 'Divine Body' (*CPP* 179; *CP* 699). This means that to 'offend' against one of the Divine Family is to offend against all, for all *are* 'Jesus the Christ'. Albion's punishment of Luvah in *Jerusalem* is, then, figured as a punishment *of* the 'Divine Body'. Thus 'Beulah', Blake's land of dreamful feminine harmony, laments over Albion's revenges: 'Why did you take Vengeance O ye Sons of the mighty Albion?/ . . . As the Sons of Albion have done to Luvah: so they have in him/ Done to the Divine Lord & Saviour' (*CPP* 170; *CP* 684).

Echoing the idiom of the revolutionary prophecies of the early 1790s (see chapter 3), Blake's *Jerusalem* overlays biblical prophecy and Christian theodicy on contemporary European politics – and conflates history and spirituality in such a way that the spiritual meaning of Britain's vengeance against France is read in terms of apocalyptic typology and antinomian ethics. David Erdman says that *Jerusalem*'s free manipulation of historical chronology in its treatment of the Napoleonic Wars effectively 'extend[s] the war over time and space and erase[s] any sense of finality from the concept of a Victory'; the result of this is that attention becomes focused on 'Albion's desire to crucify Luvah as the central issue'.[9] *Jerusalem* is, then, a work that urgently meditates

and mourns over the viciously vengeful psychology and ideology that drives Albion's actions – and that calls on Albion to rise from the spiritual death his aggression generates. Blake is concerned throughout *Jerusalem* – as in the preface to each chapter – with the *ideological* or 'spiritual' determinants of Albion's historical fate; and the Christological ethic advanced in the poem seeks decisively to *interrupt* the psychology and politics of accusation-and-punishment in European history in favour of a transformed, apocalyptic future that is modelled on the regenerative and communitarian life of 'Eden'.

Albion vengefully 'vote[s] the death of Luvah', and 'nail[s] him to Albions Tree' (*CPP* 216; *CP* 766) in 'Chap 3' of *Jerusalem*; and Erdman reads this symbolic crucifixion in terms of Britain's retributive policy towards Napoleonic France in 1814–15.[10] Luvah-France may 'sl[ay] Tharmas the Angel of the Tongue' in the repressiveness, militarism and imperialism of the post-revolutionary, Napoleonic era – but *Jerusalem* nevertheless mourns the fact that, in response, Albion brings Luvah 'To Justice in his own City of Paris, denying the Resurrection' (*CPP* 214; *CP* 761). This, evidently, is Blake's comment on the two Treaties of Paris of 1814 and 1815[11] that, either side of Napoleon's disastrous 'Hundred Days' of return from exile on Elba in 1814 and defeat at Waterloo in 1815, settled the Napoleonic Wars finally, with the reimposition of the Bourbon monarchy on France by the monarchical and imperial European powers under Louis XVIII. In Blakean terms, this is a denial of the 'Resurrection' of the 1789 Revolution in a retributive and regressive restoration of unregenerate political power.

The trauma of the 'strife of Albion & Luvah' (*CPP* 195; *CP* 727) in *Jerusalem* turns Blake's political radicalism not, as is sometimes assumed, inwards towards mysticism and quietism – but outwards and forwards into an analysis of the pathology of Albion's social body, and into projective visions of possible social and political futurity. One of the spaces of potential political liberty in *Jerusalem*, for instance, is the visionary prospect opened up by the appearance of 'Erin', for Erin in *Jerusalem* is the spiritual form of Ireland, a nation that in the early nineteenth century was shackled by 'Albion' beneath the Act of Union of Britain and Ireland in 1801, following the bloody suppression by Castlereagh of the revolt of the 'United Irishmen' against British colonial rule in 1798. In the early 1810s, Byron and Shelley were both supporters of the Irish movement for Catholic Emancipation – and, ultimately, for national liberation – under Daniel O'Connell, and Blake's *Jerusalem* likewise projects 'Erin' as a visionary form of emancipated political futurity. At the end of 'Chap 3' Blake writes: 'I see a Feminine Form arise from the Four terrible Zoas/ Beautiful but terrible struggling to take a form of beauty/ . . . this is Dinah, the youthful form of Erin . . .' (*CPP* 230; *CP* 795). Like Orc in *America*, Erin in *Jerusalem* is an image of the struggle of emancipatory political vision to find a future historical embodiment.

In the 'youthful form' of Dinah, Erin stands as a visionary figure of political futurity, and in the rhetorical sweep of *Jerusalem* so, too, does Blake's complex and anguished figure of 'Jerusalem' herself. In 'C 4' Los, labouring in the deadly night of history, sings songs and sees visions of future emancipatory possibility – in particular his vision of the 'New Jerusalem' of spiritual and social regeneration, 'descending' from heaven. Los sings:

> I see thy Form O lovely mild Jerusalem, Wingd with Six Wings
> In the opacous Bosom of the Sleeper, lovely Three-fold
> In Head & Heart & Reins, three Universes of love & beauty
> Thy forehead bright . . .
> Albion beloved land; I see thy mountains & thy hills
> And valleys & thy pleasant Cities Holiness to the Lord
> . . . I see the River of Life & Tree of Life
> I see the New Jerusalem descending out of Heaven
> Between thy Wings of gold & silver featherd immortal
> Clear as the rainbow, as the cloud of the Suns tabernacle
>
> (*CPP* 244–5; *CP* 820–21)

Seen or envisioned by Los 'In' the bosom of the sleeping Albion, Jerusalem is a permanent or perpetual *visionary possibility* in Albion's lacerated and fallen self; and Los's unremitting labour in *Jerusalem* is to persuade Albion to embrace this vision, to open himself up to the life of 'LIBERTY' (*CPP* 171; *CP* 685) that he has exiled from himself. Los, then, strives relentlessly against the 'rocky forms of Death' (*CPP* 229; *CP* 792) of history, 'demolish[ing] time on time' 'with his mighty Hammer' the confining 'Kings & Nobles of the Earth' – 'Arthur Alfred the

Norman Conqueror Richard John/ [*Edward Henry Elizabeth James Charles William George*]' (*CPP* 228; *CP* 791)[12] – in a ceaseless struggle to open up Albion's fallen body and vision to liberty and regeneration. Jerusalem herself in the poem mourns her rejection by Albion, echoing Oothoon in *Visions* and Ahania in *Ahania*; and her lamentation is framed essentially in terms of the distance, division or separation between herself and her lover, husband and friend, 'Albion'. She calls:

> How distant far from Albion! his hills & his valleys no more
> Receive the feet of Jerusalem: they have cast me quite away:
> And Albion is himself shrunk to a narrow rock in the midst of the sea!
> The plains of Sussex & Surrey, their hills of flocks & herds
> No more seek to Jerusalem nor to the sound of my Holy-ones.
> The Fifty-two Counties of England are hardend against me . . .
> London coverd the whole Earth. England encompassd the Nations:
> And all the Nations of the Earth were seen in the Cities of Albion . . .
> Medway mingled with Kishon: Thames receivd the heavenly Jordan . . .
> Italy saw me, in sublime astonishment: France was wholly mine:
> As my garden & my secret bath; Spain was my heavenly couch:
> I slept in his golden hills: the Lamb of God met me there.
>
> (*CPP* 234–5; *CP* 802–3)

In a universal vision that simultaneously mourns and reimagines a radical republic of nations, Jerusalem disperses or dissipates Albion's-Britain's aggressive and dominative imperialism; for she envisions the relation of nations in terms not of singular possession or dominion, but of interpenetrative *mutuality* – the 'Nations' inhabit one another and share each other's fraternal life as do the members of the 'Divine Body' in Eden. And 'Jerusalem' herself is the visionary embodiment of this harmony in history. In contrast to Jerusalem's inclusive vision, the divisions of Albion's imperial conflicts are materialized in the 'narrow', 'rock[y]' and 'hardend' forms of opposed and antagonistic countries and collectives; and it is to these separations and divisions in Albion's universal yet conflicted body that the ethical hero of *Jerusalem*, 'Jesus the Saviour' (*CPP* 182; *CP* 704), addresses himself in his role as the apocalyptic 'Remover of Limits' (*CPP* 228; *CP* 791). In a reimagining of his antinomian role as the dissolver of 'Law', Jesus in *Jerusalem* is figured as the transgressor of – and liberator from – every 'Limit': he is the dissolver of all bounds, separations and imprisoning divisions in language, politics, law and ideology. Suffering beneath Albion's rocky definition of her, for example, as a polluted whore or 'Harlot', Jerusalem says to the Saviour:

> A Harlot I am calld. I am sold from street to street!
> I am defaced with blows & with the dirt of the prison!
> And wilt thou become my Husband O my Lord & Saviour?
> Shall Vala bring thee forth! shall the Chaste be ashamed also?
> I see the Maternal Line, I behold the Seed of the Woman!
> . . . These are the Daughters of Vala, Mother of the Body of death
>
> (*CPP* 212–13; *CP* 759–60)

Here, Jerusalem the 'Harlot' becomes the beloved of the Saviour, and, instead of being an outcast, the harlot is given a husband. Just before this, the Saviour says to Jerusalem: 'Man in the Resurrection changes his Sexual Garments at will/ Every Harlot was once a Virgin: every Criminal an Infant Love!/ Repose on me till the morning of the Grave. I am thy life' (*CPP* 212; *CP* 759). Here, Jesus becomes an antinomian engine of symbolic 'Resurrection' that removes all 'Limits' from the pernicious, maleficent and imprisoning definitions which – like the 'mind-forg'd manacles' of 'London' (see chapter 2) – shackle humankind in historical punishment and pain. The exchange between Jerusalem and the Saviour is preceded by a beautiful reimagining of the annunciation and nativity story of Christian tradition (see *CPP* 211–12; *CP* 756–9). In Blake's version, though, the 'Virgin Mary' is *not* a virgin, but an adulteress, and what makes the annunciation of the Saviour's birth possible is the *fact that Joseph forgives her*, thus embodying or realizing in his actions the meaning and presence of forgiveness that the coming Christ child symbolizes. Vala-Babylon, the embodiment of corrupt, vicious and vengeful female sexuality in Blake, declares in the same scene: 'Does the voice of my Lord call me again? am I pure thro his Mercy/ And Pity. Am I become lovely as a Virgin in his sight who am/ Indeed a Harlot . . . does he/ Call her pure as he did in the days of her Infancy . . .' (*CPP* 212; *CP* 758). '[D]oes he/ Call her pure . . .', Vala says; for, in a regenerative renaming,

Jesus shatters the miseries of the moral law in apocalyptic, visionary, forgiving, and annihilating redefinition. The reinvention of the language of 'purity' that Oothoon fails to achieve in *Visions of the Daughters of Albion*, because of her enchainment in history, is secured by the Saviour in a projective and prophetic transformation of a benighted tradition. In response to Jerusalem's amazement that the Saviour should render the 'Chaste' 'ashamed' by embracing in love the virgin 'Vala', Jesus says, 'I am the Resurrection & the Life./ I Die & pass the limits of possibility, as it appears/ To individual perception' (*CPP* 213; *CP* 760) – and, indeed, Jesus's saving sublime in *Jerusalem is* a perpetual exceeding of the limits of sense and self, of 'possibility', in favour of symbolic transformation, reimagining, and an apocalypse of self-annihilation.

As *Jerusalem*'s climax approaches, Los presents a vision of regeneration in which the tyrannous frameworks of religious orthodoxy are, like the Saviour's exceeding of the 'limits of possibility' in language, dissolved in a play of visions without terror or power. Los envisions a time, that is, when 'we may Foresee & Avoid/ The terrors of Creation & Redemption & Judgment. Beholding them/ Displayd in the Emanative Visions of Canaan in Jerusalem & in Shiloh/ And in the Shadows of Remembrance, & in the Chaos of the Spectre' (*CPP* 252; *CP* 836). Here, the tyrannies and 'terrors' of religion's orthodox narratives of sin and punishment are 'Avoid[ed]' by their appearing only in the 'shadows of Possibility', and in 'the Vision & in the Prophecy' – they are prevented, that is, from becoming 'permanent' (*CPP* 252–3; *CP* 836) in the rocky fixities of code, creed, law or ideology. Religion's disastrous story of sin, fall and punishment is prevented from attaining hegemony in history. In the terms of *The Marriage of Heaven and Hell* (chapter 3), the 'poetic tales' of 'Creation & Redemption & Judgment' are debarred from becoming 'forms of worship' (*CPP* 38; *CP* 186) and so forms of power.

In 'Chap 3', Albion's punishing 'Warriors' declare: 'Once Man was occupied in intellectual pleasures & energies/ But now . . ./ The Feminine & Masculine Shadows soft, mild & ever varying/ In beauty: are Shadows now no more, but Rocks in Horeb' (*CPP* 222; *CP* 780). In Exodus 17:6, Moses strikes a 'rock in Horeb' in order miraculously to generate water, thus breaking fixity into fluidity; and, likewise, the 'intellectual pleasures & energies' that are lost by Albion's aggressive masculine Warriors are described as a regenerating play of shadows and fluid variations, a choreography of imaginative visions that dissolve the petrifications of law and punishment into liberatory movement. The astonishing apocalypse that ends *Jerusalem* is, then, an emancipatory *restoration* of this 'ever varying' play of intellect and imagination forfeited by Albion and his soldiers: a play that explodes poetic vision into infinitude in a limitless dance of what the poem calls 'Visionary forms dramatic' (*CPP* 257; *CP* 845). This liberation is preceded and enabled by Albion's *own* act of dissolution, or 'annihilation', of his rocky and petrific 'Selfhood cruel' (*CPP* 255; *CP* 841); for, as the 'Covering Cherub' (*CPP* 255; *CP* 842) – the avatar of all law-bound Blakean error – comes to divide Jesus away from Albion, Albion is struck with 'terror[,] not for himself but for his Friend', and gives himself for Jesus by throwing himself into 'the Furnaces of affliction' (*CPP* 256; *CP* 842). This is the narrative trigger for apocalypse, for the furnaces then 'bec[o]me/ Fountains of Living Waters flowing from the Humanity Divine' (*CPP* 255; *CP* 842–3), and Albion 'stretch[es] his hand into Infinitude' and shoots the 'Arrows of Love' and 'Arrows of Intellect' (*CPP* 256–7; *CP* 843–4) into the four compass points of an exploding, expanding, regenerating universe.

The dynamic, mobile, restless, fluid vision that is put into play at the end of *Jerusalem* is an affirmative play of the 'shadows of Possibility' described by Los, for none of these apocalyptic visions, images or elements are rockily fixed or immobile, but all are in motion and in variation. The regenerate Zoas or 'Four Faces of Humanity' (*CPP* 257; *CP* 845) are described in the following terms:

> And they conversed together in Visionary forms dramatic which bright
> Redounded from their Tongues in thunderous majesty, in Visions
> In new Expanses, creating exemplars of Memory and of Intellect
> Creating Space, Creating Time according to the wonders Divine
> Of Human Imagination, throughout all the Three Regions immense
> Of Childhood, Manhood & Old Age[;] & the all tremendous unfathomable Non Ens

Of Death was seen in regenerations terrific or complacent varying
According to the subject of discourse & every Word & Every
Character
Was Human according to the Expansion or Contraction, the
translucence or
Opakeness of Nervous fibres such was the variation of Time &
Space
Which vary according as the Organs of Perception vary & they
walked
To & fro in Eternity as One Man reflecting each in each & clearly
seen
And seeing . . .

(*CPP* 257–8; *CP* 845–6)

Here, the regenerate Zoas's 'intellectual pleasures' are both mental and political, individual and social, imaginative and material – and constitute the apocalyptic life of a community where visionary form is understood not in terms of law and fixity, but 'converse', not in terms of uniformity, but variety. It is a plural, radical republic of changing visions, determined by the restlessly multiple 'or' ('terrific *or* complacent . . . Expansion *or* Contraction . . . Translucence *or* Opakeness') of visionary forms of 'Possibility' – not by the 'One Law' of Urizenic 'Oppression' (*CPP* 44; *CP* 194). It is a flexible and fraternal life of varying visions where even the negatives of Blake's own symbolic system – for example, his unholy trinity of rational-empiricist philosophers, 'Bacon & Newton & Locke' – are incorporated in the visionary panoply of the heavens. For, along with the poets 'Milton & Shakespear & Chaucer', these thinkers' partial credos are ranged in heaven in 'The innumerable Chariots of the Almighty' (*CPP* 257; *CP* 844). It is a vision where even the 'unfathomable Non Ens/ Of Death' is seen in 'regenerations terrific *or* complacent', and the 'Body of Death' itself is submitted to an 'Eternal Death & Resurrection' (*CPP* 257; *CP* 845); for, in *Jerusalem*'s apocalypse, every vision, idea, philosophy and 'Limit' in history is submitted to 'Annihilation' (*CPP* 257; *CP* 844), and re-emerges transformed in a flexible life of imaginative 'variation'.

And it was, indeed, in terms of fluidity and motion that Blake described his own 'books' to Henry Crabb Robinson in 1826, the year before he died. Crabb Robinson writes:

his books – (& his MSS. are immense in quantity) are dictations from the Spirits – he told me yesterday that when he writes . . . he sees the words fly about the room the moment he has put them on paper And his book is then published –[13]

Notes

CHAPTER 1. LABOURING UPWARDS INTO FUTURITY: ENVISIONING WILLIAM BLAKE

1. See Martin Butlin (ed.), *The Paintings and Drawing of William Blake* (Text) (New Haven and London: Yale University Press, 1981), 140–41. Butlin says that, although the inscription 'I labour upwards into futurity Blake' is not written in Blake's hand, it 'may copy . . . an original inscription below the design matching those on other prints' (p. 141). The likelihood of this is increased by the fact that the design has been trimmed, and the motto is attributed to 'Blake'.
2. E. P. Thompson, *The Making of the English Working Class* (London: Pelican, 1968), 54–5, 56.
3. Saree Makdisi, *William Blake and the Impossible History of the 1790s* (Chicago: University of Chicago Press, 2003), 5, 10, 11.
4. See Keri Davies, 'Mrs Bliss: A Blake Collector of 1794', in Steve Clark and David Worrall (eds.), *Blake in the Nineties* (Basingstoke: Macmillan/St Martin's Press, 1999), 212–30.
5. This point is proposed in Morris Eaves, Robert N. Essick, Joseph Viscomi (eds.), *William Blake: The Early Illuminated Books* (London: William Blake Trust/Tate Gallery Publications, 1993), 114.
6. Peter Ackroyd, *Blake* (London: Sinclair-Stevenson, 1995), 60.
7. David V. Erdman, *Blake: Prophet Against Empire* (Princeton: Princeton University Press, 1977), 213.
8. For accounts of Blake's inheritance of such traditions, see Désirée Hirst, *Hidden Riches: Traditional Symbolism from the Renaissance to Blake* (London: Eyre and Spottiswoode, 1964), and Kathleen Raine, *Blake and Tradition*, 2 vols. (Princeton: Princeton University Press, 1968).
9. Though Blake did not attend a place of worship, he was baptized in an Anglican church (St James's, Piccadilly), and he evidently requested burial in Bunhill Fields, the Dissenters' burial ground,

with the service read by an Anglican clergyman. Keri Davies and Marsha Keith Schuchard (see notes 10 and 11 below) say that the Moravians '*were* and then again *were not* Dissenters . . . one could be an Anglican and a Moravian at the same time – and it turns out that a majority of the English [Moravian] brethren were and remained loyal members of the Church of England' ('Recovering the Lost Moravian History of William Blake's Family', *Blake: An Illustrated Quarterly*, 38 (2004), 36–43 (38)).

10. For an account of this schism, and of Blake's affinity with the Swedenborgian and Moravian celebration of sexuality as a conduit of spiritual experience, see Marsha Keith Schuchard, 'Why Mrs. Blake Cried: Swedenborg, Blake and the Sexual Basis of Spiritual Vision', *Esoterica*, 2 (2000), <http://www.esoteric.msu.edu>, 45–93. For a description of Blake's relationship to the New Jerusalem Church and the rifts that troubled the Church at its foundation, see E. P. Thompson, *Witness Against the Beast: William Blake and the Moral Law* (Cambridge: Cambridge University Press, 1993), 129–45.
11. One might think of such poems as 'Earth's Answer' (see chapter 2), 'The Little Girl Lost', 'The Little Girl Found', 'The Lilly', 'The Garden of Love', 'A Little Girl Lost'.
12. For this research, see Keri Davies and Marsha Keith Schuchard, 'Recovering the Lost Moravian History of William Blake's Family', *Blake: An Illustrated Quarterly*, 38 (2004), 36–43. In an earlier article, Davies made a new archival identification of Blake's mother that dismantled E. P. Thompson's speculative linking of her (in *Witness Against the Beast* 120–21) to the Muggletonians, another antinomian sect of eighteenth-century London: see Keri Davies, 'William Blake's Mother: A New Identification', *Blake: An Illustrated Quarterly*, 33 (1999), 36–50.
13. Schuchard, 'Why Mrs. Blake Cried', 47, 50. For a fascinating book-length study of the Moravian groups in Fetter Lane and Germany in this period – published after the present volume went to press – see Schuchard's, *Why Mrs Blake Cried: William Blake and the Sexual Basis of Spiritual Vision* (London: Century, 2006).
14. Schuchard, 'Why Mrs. Blake Cried', 50, 57. Schuchard says that an aspect of the split between the liberals and conservatives in the 'Swedenborg Society in 1788–90 . . . [was] the reluctance of the conservatives to publish an English translation of *Conjugal Love*' (p. 64).
15. A description of this suggestion by Schuchard and Davies is given in Matthew J. A. Green, *Visionary Materialism in the Early Works of William Blake* (Basingstoke: Palgrave Macmillan, 2005), 115.
16. Green, *Visionary Materialism*, 138. For Green's discussion of Blake's turn against Swedenborg in this period see pp. 110–15.

17. Cited in G. E. Bentley, Jr., *The Stranger from Paradise: A Biography of William Blake* (New Haven and London: Yale University Press, 2001), 181.

CHAPTER 2. RADICAL VISIONS: TRACTATES, *SONGS OF INNOCENCE AND OF EXPERIENCE*, VISIONS OF DAUGHTERS

1. Edward Larrissy, *William Blake* (Oxford: Blackwell, 1985), 36–7.
2. Jon Mee, *Dangerous Enthusiasm: William Blake and the Culture of Radicalism in the 1790s* (Oxford: Clarendon Press, 1992), 3.
3. John Locke, *An Essay Concerning Human Understanding* (1690), ed. Peter H. Nidditch (Oxford, Clarendon Press, 1975), 104.
4. Steve Clark, '"Labouring at the Resolute Anvil": Blake's Response to Locke', in Steve Clark and David Worrall (eds.), *Blake in the Nineties* (Basingstoke: Macmillan/St Martin's Press, 1999), 133–52 (135).
5. Larrissy, *William Blake*, 73.
6. Ibid., 80.
7. For a useful reading of *All Religions are One* and Enlightenment universalism, see Larrissy, *William Blake*, 71–3.
8. Wesley's hymn includes the stanzas:

    Lamb of God, I look to thee,
    Thou shalt my example be;
    Thou art gentle, meek, and mild,
    Thou wast once a little child.

    Fain I would be as thou art,
    Give me thy obedient heart;
    Thou art pitiful and kind,
    Let me have thy loving mind.
9. Heather Glen, *Vision and Disenchantment: Blake's 'Songs' and Wordsworth's 'Lyrical Ballads'* (Cambridge: Cambridge University Press, 1983), 24, 25.
10. Cited by Andrew Lincoln in Andrew Lincoln (ed.), *William Blake: 'Songs of Innocence and of Experience'* (London: William Blake Trust/Tate Gallery Publications, 1991), 159.
11. Caroline Franklin, *Mary Wollstonecraft: A Literary Life* (Basingstoke: Palgrave Macmillan, 2004), 38.
12. Glen, *Vision and Disenchantment*, 8–32.
13. Larrissy, *William Blake*, 69.
14. E. P. Thompson, *Witness Against the Beast*, 207.
15. Ibid.

16. See chapter 3 for a discussion of the language of the sublime in Blake's revolutionary prophecies.
17. Edmund Burke, *A Philosophical Enquiry into the Origins of our Ideas of the Sublime and Beautiful* (1757), ed. J. T. Boulton (London, 1958), 66.
18. Ibid.
19. Graham Pechey, '1789 and After: Mutations of "Romantic" Discourse', in *1789: Reading Writing Revolution*, ed. Frances Barker et al. (Colchester: University of Essex, 1982), 52–66 (59).
20. See, for instance, Ronald Paulson, *Representations of Revolution (1789–1820)* (New Haven and London: Yale University Press, 1983), 88–110. Paulson's chapter, 'Blake's Lamb-Tiger', gives an illuminating account of the 'sublime' language of 'counterrevolutionary polemic' (p. 108) in the period. See also Stewart Crehan's chapter, 'Blake's Tyger and the "Tygerish Multitude"', in *Blake in Context* (Dublin: Gill and Macmillan Ltd, 1984), 123–36, for a vivid '"radical", historically-based reading of "The Tyger"' as a sign of the 'terrible, new-born beauty of violent revolution' (pp. 124–5).
21. Cited in Paulson, *Representations of Revolution*, 38.
22. Ibid., 97.
23. Glen, *Vision and Disenchantment*, 209.
24. Thompson, *Witness Against the Beast*, 177.
25. Ibid., 177, 176. Thompson shows how the political ambivalence of 'chartered' freedom was a key point of dispute between Edmund Burke and Tom Paine in their ideological struggle over the French Revolution: Burke contended that liberty inhered in tradition and constitution, Paine that it resided in the idea of natural right (see pp. 177–9).
26. Raymond Williams, *The Country and the City* (London: Hogarth Press, 1973), 148.
27. For Bloom's complex but resonant intertextual reading of 'London' – and of 'The Tyger' – see his chapter 'Blake and Revisionism' in *Poetry and Repression: Revisionism from Blake to Stevens* (New Haven and London: Yale University Press, 1976), 28–51. For a discussion of Bloom's reading, see Larrissy, *William Blake*, 51–5.
28. Erdman, *Blake: Prophet Against Empire*, 214, 277.
29. Ibid., 279, 278.
30. Nelson Hilton, *Literal Imagination: Blake's Vision of Words* (California: University of California Press, 1983), 64.
31. Gerda S. Norvig, 'Female Subjectivity and the Desire of Reading In(to) Blake's *Book of Thel*', in John Lucas (ed.), *William Blake* (London and New York: Longman, 1998), 148–66 (153).
32. Helen P. Bruder, *William Blake and the Daughters of Albion* (Basingstoke and New York: Macmillan/St Martin's Press, 1997), 38–54.

33. Ibid., 41.
34. Ibid., 42.
35. Death, in fact, presides over the whole of *The Book of Thel*: on the title page, 'THE BOOK of THEL' is framed by an overarching stem that delineates the shape of a headstone, suggesting that the entire poem is about her death (*IB* 34; *CIB* 99).
36. Morris Eaves, Robert N. Essick, Joseph Viscomi (eds.), *William Blake: The Early Illuminated Books* (London: William Blake Trust/Tate Gallery Publications, 1993), 231.
37. Thirteen of the plates were signed by Blake, though several others may be by him. For a full discussion of the verbal and visual relationships between Blake's *Visions*, Wollstonecraft's *Vindication* and Stedman's *Narrative*, see my '"That Mild Beam": Enlightenment and Enslavement in William Blake's *Visions of the Daughters of Albion*', in Carl Plasa and Betty J. Ring (eds.), *The Discourse of Slavery: Aphra Behn to Toni Morrison* (London: Routledge, 1994), 40–63.
38. Stedman was a captain in the Scots Brigade, and was part of a military expedition to Dutch Guiana to suppress a slave revolt against the European planters. Though part of the suppression, Stedman deplored the atrocities he witnessed; and Erdman suggests that Stedman's divided attitude towards colonial power is reflected in Blake's Theotormon who, while mourning Oothoon's situation, colludes passively in her victimization (*Blake: Prophet Against Empire*, 233–4).
39. Mary Wollstonecraft, *A Vindication of the Rights of Woman* (1792), ed. Miriam Brody (Harmondsworth: Penguin, 1985), 130.
40. Ibid., 131.
41. For an insightful discussion of the historical impasses of Oothoon's affirmation of her desire – due to the fact that female sexual assertion was equated with whoredom at the end of the eighteenth century – see Bruder, *William Blake and the Daughters of Albion*, 55–89.
42. S. Foster Damon, *William Blake: His Philosophy and Symbols* (London: Constable, 1924), 329.

CHAPTER 3. REVOLUTIONARY PROPHECIES: *THE MARRIAGE OF HEAVEN AND HELL, AMERICA: A PROPHECY, EUROPE: A PROPHECY*

1. Alexander Gilchrist, *The Life of William Blake* (London, 1863 and 1880), 93.
2. Most notably suggested in Erdman, *Blake: Prophet Against Empire*, 152 n. 7, 192.

3. Morris Eaves, Robert N. Essick, Joseph Viscomi (eds.), *William Blake: The Early Illuminated Books* (London: William Blake Trust/Tate Gallery Publications, 1993), 114–15.
4. Thomas Paine, *The Complete Writings of Thomas Paine*, ed. P. S. Foner, 2 vols. (New York: Citadel Press, 1945), ii. 477.
5. The parallel is pointed to by Graham Pechey, '*The Marriage of Heaven and Hell*: A Text and its Conjuncture', *Oxford Literary Review*, 3:3 (1979), 52–76 (67).
6. Erdman, *Blake: Prophet Against Empire*, 181.
7. For a discussion of Blake's critique of Burke's politics and aesthetics of the 'sublime' in his revolutionary prophecies, see my *Blake's Poetry: Spectral Visions* (Basingstoke: Macmillan, 1993), 20–47.
8. David Bindman, '"My own mind is my own church": Blake, Paine and the French Revolution', in Alison Yarrington and Kelvin Everest (eds.), *Reflections of Revolution: Images of Romanticism* (London: Routledge, 1993), 112–33 (114).
9. Detlef W. Dörrbecker (ed.), *William Blake: The Continental Prophecies* (London: William Blake Trust/Tate Gallery Publications, 1995), 17.
10. Mee, *Dangerous Enthusiasm*, 38.
11. David E. James, 'Angels out of the Sun: Art, Religion and Politics in Blake's *America*', in David Punter (ed.), *William Blake: Contemporary Critical Essays* (Basingstoke: Macmillan, 1996), 54–70 (63).
12. Makdisi, *William Blake and the Impossible History of the 1790s*, 31.
13. Terry Eagleton, Editor's Preface, in Larrissy, *William Blake*, xi.
14. Makdisi says of Washington's speech about the 'work-bruis'd' hands and 'bleeding' feet (*CPP* 52; *CP* 210) of the Americans in *America*: 'We are ... not only *not* dealing here with the work performed by Washington and Thomas Jefferson and company, but on the contrary with the work performed by the slaves *owned* by them and the other leaders of the American war' (*William Blake and the Impossible History of the 1790s*, 33).
15. Karl Marx and Friedrich Engels, 'The Communist Manifesto' (1848), in David McLellan (ed.), *Karl Marx: Selected Writings* (Oxford: Oxford University Press, 1977), 221.
16. This point is made by Paulson, *Representations of Revolution*, 102–3.
17. Bruder, *William Blake and the Daughters of Albion*, 159.
18. For an interesting reading of the figure of Enitharmon in *Europe* that relates her to the contradictions of late eighteenth-century gender ideology and to the historical figure of Marie Antionette, the queen of France at the outbreak of the French Revolution, see Bruder, *William Blake and the Daughters of Albion*, 133–78.
19. Erdman, *Blake: Prophet Against Empire*, 211.

CHAPTER 4. BIBLES OF HELL: *THE SONG OF LOS, THE [FIRST] BOOK OF URIZEN, THE BOOK OF LOS, THE BOOK OF AHANIA*

1. Mee, *Dangerous Enthusiasm*, 124.
2. Tilottama Rajan, '(Dis)figuring the System: Vision, History and Trauma in Blake's Lambeth Books', *Huntington Library Quarterly*, 58.3 and 4 (1996), 383–411 (387).
3. Tilottama Rajan, *The Supplement of Reading: Figures of Understanding in Romantic Theory and Practice* (Ithaca and London: Cornell University Press, 1990), 254.
4. See Robert N. Essick, 'William Blake, Thomas Paine, and Biblical Revolution', *Studies in Romanticism*, 30 (1991), 189–212 (205–6).
5. Mee, *Dangerous Enthusiasm*, 170, 176.
6. Frederick E. Pierce, 'Etymology as Explanation in Blake', *Philological Quarterly*, 10 (1931), 395–9 (396). For further commentary on the punning ironies of Urizen's name around the ideas of reason, rising, origin and framing, see my 'Framing Los(s): Blake, Kant, Derrida', *Q/W/E/R/T/Y*, 5 (1995), 119–20.
7. Larrissy, *William Blake*, 128, 129.
8. David Worrall (ed.), *William Blake: The Urizen Books* (London: William Blake Trust/Tate Gallery Publications, 1995), 33.
9. Ibid., 12.
10. Ibid., 136.
11. Erdman, *Blake: Prophet Against Empire*, 315.
12. David Erdman (ed.), *The Illuminated Blake* (Oxford: Oxford University Press, 1975), 213.
13. Erdman, *Blake: Prophet Against Empire*, 315.
14. See Worrall, *The Urizen Books*, 162–3.
15. Mee, *Dangerous Enthusiasm*, 206.
16. Ibid., 201.
17. Worrall, *The Urizen Books*, 221.

CHAPTER 5. CONTEMPORARY EPICS: *'VALA', OR 'THE FOUR ZOAS', MILTON: A POEM*

1. G. E. Bentley, Jr., *The Stranger from Paradise: A Biography of William Blake* (New Haven and London: Yale University Press, 2001), 9.
2. Steve Clark and David Worrall (eds.), *Historicizing Blake* (Basingstoke: Macmillan/St Martin's Press, 1994), 11.

3. Facsimile editions of the text are: G. E. Bentley Jr. (ed.), *'Vala', or 'The Four Zoas': A Facsimile of the Manuscript, a Transcript of the Poem, and a Study of Its Growth and Significance* (Oxford: Clarendon Press, 1963); and Cettina Tramontano Magno and David V. Erdman (eds.), *'The Four Zoas' by William Blake: A Photographic Facsimile of the Manuscript with Commentary on the Illuminations* (Lewisburg, PA: Bucknell University Press; London: Associated University Presses, 1987).
4. Erdman, *Blake: Prophet Against Empire*, 401.
5. Ibid., 317.
6. Robert N. Essick and Morton D. Paley, '"Dear Generous Cumberland": A Newly Discovered Letter and Poem by William Blake', *Blake: An Illustrated Quarterly*, 32 (1998), 4–13 (4, 5).
7. Jon Mee, 'Blake's politics in history', in Morris Eaves (ed.), *The Cambridge Companion to William Blake* (Cambridge: Cambridge University Press, 2003), 133–49 (145).
8. Cited in G. E. Bentley, Jr., *Blake Records* (Oxford: Clarendon Press, 1969), 42.
9. Lucy Newlyn, *'Paradise Lost' and the Romantic Reader* (Oxford: Clarendon Press, 1993), 272.
10. Robert N. Essick and Joseph Viscomi (eds.), *William Blake: 'Milton a Poem' and the Final Illuminated Works: 'The Ghost of Abel', 'On Homers Poetry [and] On Virgil', 'Laocoön'* (London: William Blake Trust/Tate Gallery Publications, 1995), 16.
11. Cited in Florence Sandler, 'The Iconoclastic Enterprise: Blake's Critique of "Milton's Religion"', in Nelson Hilton (ed.), *Essential Articles for the Study of William Blake, 1970–1984* (Hamden, CT: Archon Books, 1986), 33–55 (37).
12. Blake's visual depictions of Milton in *Milton*, of course, present the 'Human' Milton, naked – for instance, as he sunders his own name in self-revision on the title page (*IB* 217; *CIB* 246), divests himself of the 'robe of the promise' (*CPP* 108; *CP* 539) before leaving heaven (*IB* 232; *CIB* 260), and annihilates his Urizenic 'Selfhood' in regeneration (*IB* 234; *CIB* 262). Ololon's virgin form, and subsequent sexual union with Milton, is a rewriting of the chaste 'Lady' of Milton's *Comus* (1637), and a revaluation of Milton's negative portrayals of femininity elsewhere – such as Eve as a temptress in *Paradise Lost* (1674), or Dalila as a sexual seductress in *Samson Agonistes* (1671).
13. Essick and Viscomi, *William Blake: 'Milton a Poem'*, 210.

14. The revelatory nature of this 'Garment' refers to the 'book ... written within and without' of Ezekiel 2:10, and to the Messiah's 'book written within and on the backside' of Revelation 5:1, while Milton's and Ololon's consummation reconfigures the account of the marriage of the Lamb with his bride in Revelation 19, where the Saviour is clothed 'with a vesture dipped in blood' (verse 13).

CHAPTER 6. SOCIAL EPIC: *JERUSALEM: THE EMANATION OF THE GIANT ALBION*

1. Blake left this lyric untitled, but it has since become known as 'Jerusalem' through Charles Parry's popular musical setting. The fact that the poem, set to Parry's rousing melody, is sung as a nationalist hymn alongside 'Land of Hope and Glory' and 'Rule Britannia' at the Last Night of the Proms at the Royal Albert Hall each year, and was appropriated by the British Conservative Party at their pre-election press conferences after the 1982 Falklands War, is a sad political irony in the light of Blake's fierce anti-imperialism.
2. Bentley, *Blake Records*, 187.
3. Ibid., 229.
4. Morton D. Paley (ed.), *William Blake: 'Jerusalem The Emanation of the Giant Albion'* (London: William Blake Trust/Tate Gallery Publications, 1991), 12. For the Jerome McGann commentary to which Paley refers, see McGann, 'William Blake Illuminates the Truth', *Critical Studies*, 1 (1989), 43–60. For a reading of *Jerusalem* Plate 3 in the context of Blake's aesthetics of the 'sublime', see my 'Blake's Material Sublime', *Studies in Romanticism*, 41 (2002), 237–57.
5. Robert N. Essick, '*Jerusalem* and Blake's final works', in Morris Eaves (ed.), *The Cambridge Companion to William Blake* (Cambridge: Cambridge University Press, 2003), 251–71 (253).
6. This is Gilchrist's title for Chapter XXVII of his *The Life of William Blake.*
7. Bentley, *Blake Records*, 216.
8. The magistrates who indicted Blake in October 1803 were John Quantock ('Kwantok'), John Peachey ('Peachey') and William Brereton ('Brereton'); the lieutenant who presented the Bill of Indictment was George Hulton ('Hutton'); the soldiers who jointly accused Blake were John Scholfield ('Scofield!') and John Cock ('Kox').
9. Erdman, *Blake: Prophet Against Empire*, 467.
10. See ibid., 462–3, 466–7.

11. Ibid., 466.
12. The italicized line of monarchs, leading up to Blake's period with 'George', is erased; Morton D. Paley comments that this may be the result of 'second thoughts in a man who had once been tried for sedition' (*William Blake: 'Jerusalem The Emanation of the Giant Albion'* 253).
13. Bentley, *Blake Records*, 324.

Select Bibliography

EDITIONS OF WORKS BY BLAKE

Editions of Blake's Writings

Ostriker, Alicia (ed.), *William Blake: The Complete Poems* (Harmondsworth: Penguin, 1977).
Bentley, G. E., Jr. (ed.), *William Blake's Writings*, 2 vols. (Oxford: Clarendon Press, 1977).
Johnson, Mary Lynn, and John E. Grant (eds.), *Blake's Poetry and Designs* (New York: Norton, 1979).
Keynes, Geoffrey (ed.), *Blake: Complete Writings with Variant Readings* (Oxford: Oxford University Press, 1979).
Erdman, David V. (ed.), *The Complete Poetry and Prose of William Blake* (New York: Doubleday, 1988).
Stevenson, W. H. (ed.), *Blake: The Complete Poems* (London and New York: Longman, 1989).
Fuller, David (ed.), *William Blake: Selected Poetry and Prose* (London and New York: Longman, 2000).

Editions and Facsimiles of Blake's Illuminated and Graphic Works

Bentley, G. E., Jr. (ed.), *'Vala', or 'The Four Zoas': A Facsimile of the Manuscript, a Transcript of the Poem, and a Study of Its Growth and Significance* (Oxford: Clarendon Press, 1963).
Erdman, David V., *The Notebook of William Blake: A Photographic and Typographic Facsimile* (Oxford: Clarendon Press, 1973).
Keynes, Geoffrey (ed.), *The Marriage of Heaven and Hell* (London and New York: Oxford University Press, 1975).
—— *Songs of Innocence and of Experience* (London and New York: Oxford University Press, 1977).

Bindman, David (ed.), *The Complete Graphic Works of William Blake* (London: Thames and Hudson; New York: Putnam, 1978).

Easson, Kay Parkhurst, and Roger R. Easson (eds.), *The Book of Urizen* (New York: Random House, 1978).

—— *Milton* (New York: Random House, 1978).

Butlin, Martin (ed.), *The Paintings and Drawing of William Blake*, 2 vols. (New Haven and London: Yale University Press, 1981).

Erdman, David V., and Cettina Tramontano Magno (eds.), *'The Four Zoas' by William Blake: A Photographic Facsimile of the Manuscript with Commentary on the Illuminations* (Lewisburg, PA: Bucknell University Press; London: Associated University Presses, 1987).

Essick, Robert N., *William Blake's Commercial Book Illustrations: A Catalogue and Study of the Plates Engraved by Blake after Designs by Other Artists* (Oxford: Clarendon Press, 1991).

Paley, Morton D. (ed.), *William Blake: 'Jerusalem The Emanation of the Giant Albion'* (London: William Blake Trust/Tate Gallery Publications, 1991).

Lincoln, Andrew (ed.), *William Blake: 'Songs of Innocence and of Experience'* (London: William Blake Trust/Tate Gallery Publications, 1991).

Erdman, David V. (ed.), *The Illuminated Blake* (1974; New York: Dover Publications, 1992).

Eaves, Morris, Robert N. Essick and Joseph Viscomi (eds.), *William Blake: The Early Illuminated Books* (London: William Blake Trust/Tate Gallery Publications, 1993).

Dörrbecker, Detlef W. (ed.), *William Blake: The Continental Prophecies* (London: William Blake Trust/Tate Gallery Publications, 1995).

Worrall, David (ed.), *William Blake: The Urizen Books* (London: William Blake Trust/Tate Gallery Publications, 1995).

Essick, Robert N., and Joseph Viscomi (eds.), *William Blake: 'Milton a Poem' and the Final Illuminated Works: 'The Ghost of Abel', 'On Homers Poetry [and] On Virgil', 'Laocoön'* (London: William Blake Trust/Tate Gallery Publications, 1995).

Bindman, David (ed.), *William Blake: The Complete Illuminated Books* (London: Thames and Hudson, 2001).

Scholarly Internet Resources

Eaves, Morris, Robert N. Essick and Joseph Viscomi (eds.), *The William Blake Archive* <http://www.blakearchive.org>.

Hilton, Nelson (ed.), *Blake Digital Text Project* <http://www.english.uga.edu/wblake>.

BIBLIOGRAPHY

Bentley, G. E., Jr., *Blake Books: Annotated Catalogues of William Blake's Writings in Illuminated Printing, in Conventional Typography and in Manuscript* (Oxford: Clarendon Press, 1977).
—— *Blake Books Supplement* (Oxford: Clarendon Press, 1995).
'Blake and His Circle: A Checklist of Recent Scholarship', *Blake/An Illustrated Quarterly* (annually updated).

DICTIONARIES AND CONCORDANCES

Damon, S. Foster, *A Blake Dictionary: The Ideas and Symbols of William Blake* (1965; Hanover, NH: University Press of New England, 1988).
Erdman, David V., *A Concordance to the Writings of William Blake*, 2 vols. (Ithaca, NY: Cornell University Press, 1967).

PERIODICALS

Blake/An Illustrated Quarterly.

BIOGRAPHY

Ackroyd, Peter, *Blake* (London: Sinclair-Stevenson, 1995).
Bentley, G. E., Jr., *Blake Records* (Oxford: Clarendon Press, 1969).
—— *Blake Records Supplement* (Oxford: Clarendon Press, 1988).
—— *The Stranger from Paradise: A Biography of William Blake* (New Haven and London: Yale University Press, 2001).
Gilchrist, Alexander, *The Life of William Blake, Pictor Ignotus* (1863; New York: Dover, 1998).
King, James, *William Blake: His Life* (London: Weidenfeld and Nicolson, 1991).
Wilson, Mona, *The Life of William Blake* (1927; Oxford: Oxford University Press, 1971).

CRITICISM

Adams, Hazard (ed.), *Critical Essays on William Blake* (Boston, MA: G. K. Hall, 1991).
Ault, Donald, *Visionary Physics: Blake's Response to Newton* (Chicago: Chicago University Press, 1974).

—— *Narrative Unbound: Re-Visioning William Blake's 'The Four Zoas'* (Barrytown: Station Hill Press, 1987).

Behrendt, Stephen C., *Reading William Blake* (London, New York: Macmillan/St Martin's Press, 1992).

Bentley, G. E., Jr. (ed.), *William Blake: The Critical Heritage* (Boston: Routledge & Kegan Paul, 1975).

Bindman, David, *Blake as an Artist* (Oxford: Phaidon, 1977).

—— *William Blake: His Art and Times* (London: Oxford University Press, 1982).

Bloom, Harold, *Blake's Apocalypse: A Study in Poetic Argument* (New York: Doubleday, 1963).

Bracher, Mark, *Being Form'd: Thinking Through Blake's 'Milton'* (Barrytown: Station Hill Press, 1985).

Bruder, Helen P., *William Blake and the Daughters of Albion* (Basingstoke: Macmillan/St Martin's Press, 1997).

Clark, Lorraine, *Blake, Kierkegaard, and the Spectre of Dialectic* (Cambridge: Cambridge University Press, 1991).

Clark, Steve and David Worrall (eds.), *Historicizing Blake* (Basingstoke: Macmillan/St Martin's Press, 1994).

—— *Blake in the Nineties* (Basingstoke: Macmillan/St Martin's Press, 1999).

Connolly, Tristanne, *William Blake and the Body* (Basingstoke: Palgrave Macmillan, 2002).

Crehan, Stewart, *Blake in Context* (Dublin: Gill and Macmillan Ltd, 1984).

Curran, Stuart, and Joseph Anthony Wittreich, Jr. (eds.), *Blake's Sublime Allegory: Essays on 'The Four Zoas', 'Milton', and 'Jerusalem'* (Madison: University of Wisconsin Press, 1973).

Damon, S. Foster, *William Blake: His Philosophy and Symbols* (London: Constable, 1924).

Damrosch, Leopold, Jr., *Symbol and Truth in Blake's Myth* (Princeton: Princeton University Press, 1980).

Dent, Shirley, and Jason Whittaker, *Radical Blake: Afterlife and Influence from 1827* (Basingstoke: Palgrave Macmillan, 2003).

DiSalvo, Jacqueline, *War of Titans: Blake's Critique of Milton and the Politics of Religion* (Pittsburgh: University of Pittsburgh Press, 1983).

DiSalvo, Jacqueline, George A. Rosso, Jr., and Christopher Z. Hobson (eds.), *Blake, Politics and History* (New York: Garland Publishing, 1998).

Dorfman, Deborah, *Blake in the Nineteenth Century: His Reputation as a Poet from Gilchrist to Yeats* (New Haven: Yale University Press, 1969).

Eaves, Morris, *William Blake's Theory of Art* (Princeton: Princeton University Press, 1982).

—— (ed.), *The Cambridge Companion to William Blake* (Cambridge: Cambridge University Press, 2003).

Erdman, David V., *Blake: Prophet Against Empire* (Princeton: Princeton University Press, 1977).

Essick, Robert, *William Blake, Printmaker* (Princeton: Princeton University Press, 1980).

Ferber, Michael, *The Social Vision of William Blake* (Guildford: Princeton University Press, 1985).

—— *The Poetry of William Blake* (London: Penguin; New York: Viking, 1991).

Fox, Susan, *Poetic Form in Blake's 'Milton'* (Princeton: Princeton University Press, 1976).

Frye, Northrop, *Fearful Symmetry: A Study of William Blake* (1947; Princeton: Princeton University Press, 1969).

Fuller, David, *Blake's Heroic Argument* (London: Croom Helm, 1988).

Gallant, Christine, *Blake and the Assimilation of Chaos* (Princeton: Princeton University Press, 1978).

George, Diana Hume, *Blake and Freud* (Ithaca, NY: Cornell University Press, 1980).

Glausser, Wayne, *Locke and Blake: A Conversation Across the Eighteenth Century* (Gainesville: University Press of Florida, 1998).

Glen, Heather, *Vision and Disenchantment: Blake's 'Songs' and Wordsworth's 'Lyrical Ballads'* (Cambridge: Cambridge University Press, 1983).

Green, Matthew J. A., *Visionary Materialism in the Early Works of William Blake* (Basingstoke: Palgrave Macmillan, 2005).

Hamlyn, Robin and Michael Phillips (eds.), *William Blake* (London: Tate Gallery; New York: Abrams, 2000).

Hilton, Nelson (ed.), *Essential Articles for the Study of William Blake, 1970–1984* (Hamden, CT: Archon Books, 1986).

—— *Literal Imagination: Blake's Vision of Words* (California: University of California Press, 1983).

Hilton, Nelson, and Thomas A. Vogler, *Unnam'd Forms: Blake and Textuality* (Berkeley: University of California Press, 1986).

Hirst, Désirée, *Hidden Riches: Traditional Symbolism from the Renaissance to Blake* (London: Eyre and Spottiswoode, 1964).

Hobson, Christopher Z., *Blake and Homosexuality* (Basingstoke: Palgrave Macmillan, 2000).

Hutchings, Kevin, *Imagining Nature: Blake's Environmental Poetics* (Montreal: McGill-Queen's University Press, 2002).

Larrissy, Edward, *William Blake* (Oxford: Blackwell, 1985).

Leader, Zachary, *Reading Blake's 'Songs'* (London: Routledge & Kegan Paul, 1981).

Lincoln, Andrew, *A Spiritual History: A Reading of William Blake's 'Vala', or 'The Four Zoas'* (Oxford: Clarendon Press, 1995).

Luca, Vincent A. de, *Words of Eternity: Blake and the Poetics of the Sublime* (Princeton: Princeton University Press, 1991).

Lucas, John (ed.), *William Blake* (London and New York: Longman, 1998).

Makdisi, Saree, *William Blake and the Impossible History of the 1790s* (Chicago: University of Chicago Press, 2003).

Mee, Jon, *Dangerous Enthusiasm: William Blake and the Culture of Radicalism in the 1790s* (Oxford: Clarendon Press, 1992).

Miller, Dan, Mark Bracher and Donald Ault (eds.), *Critical Paths: Blake and the Argument of Method* (Durham, NC: Duke University Press, 1987).

Mitchell, W. J. T., *Blake's Composite Art: A Study of the Illuminated Poetry* (Princeton: Princeton University Press, 1978).

Moskal, Jeanne, *Blake, Ethics, and Forgiveness* (Alabama: University of Alabama Press, 1994).

Newlyn, Lucy, *'Paradise Lost' and the Romantic Reader* (Oxford: Clarendon Press, 1993).

Paley, Morton D., *Energy and the Imagination: A Study of the Development of Blake's Thought* (Oxford: Clarendon Press, 1970).

—— *The Continuing City: William Blake's 'Jerusalem'* (Oxford: Clarendon Press, 1983).

Phillips, Michael (ed.), *Interpreting Blake* (Cambridge: Cambridge University Press, 1978).

Punter, David, *Blake, Hegel and Dialectic* (Amsterdam: Rodopi, 1982).

—— (ed.), *William Blake: Contemporary Critical Essays* (Basingstoke: Macmillan, 1996).

Otto, Peter, *Constructive Vision and Visionary Deconstruction: Los, Eternity, and the Productions of Time in the Later Poetry of William Blake* (Oxford: Clarendon Press, 1991).

—— *Blake's Critique of Transcendence: Love, Jealousy, and the Sublime in 'The Four Zoas'* (Oxford: Oxford University Press, 2000).

Raine, Kathleen, *Blake and Tradition*, 2 vols. (Princeton: Princeton University Press, 1968).

—— *William Blake* (London: Thames & Hudson, 1970).

Rothenberg, Molly Ann, *Rethinking Blake's Textuality* (Columbia and London: University of Missouri Press, 1993).

Sabri-Tabrizi, G. R., *The 'Heaven' and 'Hell' of William Blake* (London: Lawrence & Wishart, 1973).

Schuchard, Marsha Keith, *Why Mrs Blake Cried: William Blake and the Sexual Basis of Spiritual Vision* (London: Century, 2006).

Tannenbaum, Leslie, *Biblical Tradition in Blake's Early Prophecies: The Great Code of Art* (Princeton: Princeton University Press, 1982).

Thompson, E. P., *Witness Against the Beast: William Blake and the Moral Law* (Cambridge: Cambridge University Press, 1993).

Vine, Steven, *Blake's Poetry: Spectral Visions* (Basingstoke: Macmillan, 1993).

Viscomi, Joseph, *Blake and the Idea of the Book* (Chichester: Princeton University Press, 1993).

Warner, Janet, *Blake and the Language of Art* (Montreal: McGill-Queen's University Press, 1984).

Webster, Brenda S., *Blake's Prophetic Psychology* (Stanford: Stanford University Press, 1983).

Williams, Nicholas, *Ideology and Utopia in the Poetry of William Blake* (Cambridge: Cambridge University Press, 1998).

—— (ed.), *Palgrave Advances in William Blake Studies* (Basingstoke: Palgrave Macmillan, 2005).

Wittreich, Joseph Anthony, Jr., *Angel of Apocalypse: Blake's Idea of Milton* (Madison: University of Wisconsin Press, 1975).

Index

Ackroyd, Peter, 7
American Revolution, 35, 39, 46, 47, 49, 51, 57
Amiens, Peace of, 81
Antionette, Marie, 31, 116 n18
Armitage, Catherine (née Wright: WB's mother), 8
Armitage, Thomas, 8

Bacon, Francis, 109
Berkeley, George, 3
Bindman, David, 46
Blake, Catherine (WB's wife), 8, 85, 94
Blake, James (WB's father), 8
Blake, William
  All Religions are One, 14, 16, 18, 100, 113 n7
  America, 6, 35, 46–52, 59, 61, 71, 83, 104
  'Ancient of Days', 53
  The Book of Ahania, 61, 62, 69–74, 76, 78, 80, 82, 83, 89, 104
  The Book of Los, 61, 74–8, 80, 82
  The Book of Thel, 32–5, 115 n35
  The [First] Book of Urizen, 1, 61–9, 71, 76, 77, 78, 89, 99
  For Children: the Gates of Paradise, 4
  A Descriptive Catalogue, 51, 96, 98
  Europe, 6, 7, 48, 52–8, 59, 61, 83, 99
  The French Revolution, 4, 46
  An Island in the Moon, 12
  Jerusalem, 2, 4, 80, 83, 95–110
  The Marriage of Heaven and Hell, 6, 8, 9, 15, 40–6, 47, 55, 56, 60, 63, 64, 65, 75, 78, 87, 88, 89, 107
  Milton, 3, 78, 80, 86, 87–94, 95, 96, 118 n12
  A Small Book of Designs, 1
  The Song of Los, 59–61, 75, 80, 83
  Songs of Innocence and of Experience, 6, 8, 15–32, 95
    'A Little Girl Lost', 112 n11
    'The Chimney Sweeper', 30
    'The Divine Image', 16–18, 22, 25
    'Earth's Answer', 20–2, 25, 112 n11
    'The Garden of Love', 112 n11
    'The Human Abstract', 22–3, 33
    'Introduction' (*Experience*), 20–2
    'Introduction' (*Innocence*), 18–20
    'The Lamb', 15–16, 23, 25
    'The Lilly', 112 n11
    'The Little Girl Found', 112 n11
    'The Little Girl Lost', 112 n11
    'London', 27–32, 106, 114 n27
    'The Tyger', 23–7, 114 n27
  There is No Natural Religion, 5, 12–14, 33
  'Vala', or *'The Four Zoas'*, 20, 80–6, 88, 89, 96
  Visions of the Daughters of Albion, 8, 21, 32, 35–8, 55, 57, 73, 104, 107
Bloom, Harold, 29, 114 n27
Bonaparte, Napoleon, 83, 90, 101, 103
Boswell, James, 28
Brereton, William, 119 n8
Bruder, Helen, 33, 34, 53, 115 n41, 116 n18
Burke, Edmund, 23–24, 27, 44–5, 114 n25

A Philosophical Enquiry into the Origins of our Ideas of the Sublime and Beautiful, 23–4, 44–5
Butts, Thomas, 85
Byron, Lord George Gordon, 104

Castlereagh, Lord, 103
Charles I, 92
Charles II, 3
Chaucer, Geoffrey, 109
Clark, Steve, 14
Cock, John, 119 n8
Crabb Robinson, Henry, 109
Crehan, Stewart, 114, n20
Cumberland, George, 86, 95

Damon, S. Foster, 37
Davies, Keri, 8, 9, 112 n9, 112 n12
Defoe, Daniel, 28
Derrida, Jacques, 11
Dörrbecker, Detlef, 47

Eagleton, Terry, 49
East India Company, 28, 29
Engels, Friedrich, 50
Erdman, David, 7, 30, 31, 45, 58, 70, 71, 83, 102, 103, 115 n38, 116 n2
Essick, Robert, 63, 91, 98
Examiner, The, 98

Falklands War, 119 n1
Flaxman, John, 39, 80, 81, 86
Franklin, Caroline, 18
Frederick the Great, 100
French Revolution, 27, 30, 31, 39, 40, 41, 45, 52–3, 56, 58, 62, 69, 70, 74, 86, 103, 116 n18

George III, 7, 51, 62
Gilchrist, Alexander, 88, 98
Gillray, James, 7
Glen, Heather, 15, 19, 28
Godwin, William, 4, 5
An Enquiry Concerning Political Justice, 4
Green, Matthew J. A., 9, 112 n15

Hayley, William, 1, 39, 86, 87, 91
Hirst, Désirée, 111 n8
Hulton, George, 119 n8
Hunt, John, 98
Hunt, Leigh, 98
Hunt, Robert, 98

James, David E., 47
Johnson, Joseph, 4, 6, 80
Johnson, Samuel, 28

Larrissy, Edward, 11, 14, 21, 65
Levi–Strauss, Claude, 11
Locke, John, 12, 13, 14, 109
An Essay Concerning Human Understanding, 12
London Swedenborg Society, 8, 112 n14
Louis XVI, 31, 40, 100
Louis XVIII, 103

Makdisi, Saree, 5, 49, 116 n14
Marx, Karl, 44, 50
McGann, Jerome, 119 n4
Mee, Jon, 11, 64, 76, 77, 86, 87
Michaelangelo, 7
Milton, John, 3, 8, 54, 70, 78, 87, 88, 90, 91, 109, 118 n12
Comus, 118 n12
'On the Morning of Christ's Nativity', 56
Paradise Lost, 54, 87, 88, 89, 92, 94, 119 n12
Samson Agonistes, 119 n12
Moravians, 8, 9, 112 n9, 112 n10, 112 n12, 112 n13
More, Hannah, 33
Essays on Various Subjects, Principally Designed for Young Ladies, 33

New Jerusalem Church, 8, 112 n10
Newlyn, Lucy, 90–1
Newton, Isaac, 109

O'Connell, Daniel, 104

Quantock, John, 119 n8

Raine, Kathleen, 111 n8
Rajan, Tilottama, 61–2
Raphael, 7
Reynolds, Sir Joshua, 2, 11, 12, 101
  Discourses on Art, 11, 101
Romilly, Sir Samuel, 27
Robespierre, Maximilien de, 46, 62, 63, 70, 71, 90
Rousseau, Jean-Jacques, 62

Scholfield, John, 99, 119 n8
Southey, Robert, 96
Schuchard, Marsha Keith, 8.9. 112 n9, 112 n10
Shakespeare, William, 109
Shelley, Percy Bysshe, 104
Stedman, John Gabriel, 36, 37, 115 n38
  Narrative, of a Five Years' Expedition, against the Revolted Negroes of Surinam, 36
Swedenborg, Emanuel, 8, 9, 40, 41, 112 n16
  The Delights of Wisdom Concerning Conjugal Love, 36, 37

Terror, Reign of, 46, 58, 62
Thompson, E. P., 3, 22, 28, 112 n10, 112 n12, 114 n25
Trusler, Dr John, 10

Union, Act of, 103

Vine, Steve, 115 n37, 116 n7, 117 n6, 119 n4
Viscomi, Joseph, 91
Voltaire, François-Marie Arouet, 62

Wakefield, Rev. Gilbert, 80
Waterloo, Battle of, 101, 103
Watson, Bishop Richard, 79, 80, 82, 86
  Apology for the Bible, 79
Watts, Isaac, 6, 17, 19
  Divine Songs, 17
  'Praise for the Gospel', 18
Wesley, Charles, 6, 15, 19, 113 n8
  'Gentle Jesus, Meek and Mild', 15, 113 n8
Williams, Raymond, 29
Wollstonecraft, Mary, 4, 36, 37, 55
  A Vindication of the Rights of Woman, 4, 36, 37, 55
Worrall, David, 66, 69, 77
Wordsworth, William, 88
  'London, 1802', 88

Young, Edward, 80
  Night Thoughts, 80

Zinzendorf, Count Nicolaus Ludwig von, 9